Revisiting Shakespeare's Tragedies

Ritu Saluja

ATLANTIC

PUBLISHERS & DISTRIBUTORS (P) LTD

Published by

ATLANTIC

PUBLISHERS & DISTRIBUTORS (P) LTD

7èk22, Ansari Road, Darya Ganj, New Delhi-110002
Phones : +91-11-40775252, 23273880, 23275880, 23280451
Fax : +91-11-23285873
Web : www.atlanticbooks.com
E-mail : orders@atlanticbooks.com

Branch Office
5, Nallathambi Street, Wallajah Road, Chennai-600002
Phones : +91-44-64611085, 32413319
E-mail : chennai@atlanticbooks.com

ISBN 978-81-269-1926-0

Printed in India at Glorious Printers, A-13, D.S.I.D.C., Jhilmil Industrial Area, Delhi-110095

Preface

Shakespeare resides in a huge, mighty and elegant world of his own. The moment we enter into his vast and endless realms, our eyes are dazzled and soul gets enlightened. Millions of beauties are poured at once on the mind's eye and along with beauties, come the ambiguities, confusion of pleasing objects, unresolved issues, false dichotomies and still unexplored areas. This continuous parade of pleasing and disturbing elements must be eyed distinctly in order to understand the true worth of the Bard.

Literary theory explains what has been hitherto mysterious or mystified about Shakespeare's texts. This book presents my entry point into the tragedies of Shakespeare by revisiting them in the light of present-day theorization. It attempts to view Shakespeare's tragedies through the prism of new critical approaches, which have proliferated since the 1960s, such as formalism, structuralism, deconstruction, Freudian psychoanalysis, feminism, Marxism, new historicism, and post-colonial theory.

Re-reading of a text clarifies meanings hitherto undelivered that go unobserved and unnoticed by the readers and audience of a particular social milieu. The book talks about multivocality in Shakespeare's tragedies by including a generous selection of earlier commentary, and is designed to represent the continuities as well as significant departures between the recent and traditional interpretations of Shakespeare's tragedies. It inevitably, reflects the intense current interest in Shakespeare.

I am thankful to everyone at Atlantic Publishers and Distributors Pvt. Ltd., New Delhi for their professionalism and helpfulness, especially Mr. Harjeet Singh who has been there from the beginning. My thanks also go to my friends and family members who helped me in every possible way.

Ritu Saluja

Contents

Introduction

When Shakespearean scholars and literary theorists are read in the effort to gain an understanding of the current trends in Shakespearean studies and literary criticism some theoretical and practical questions emerge which trouble scholars and critics: Do we need to try to define the importance of thinking deep and hard in Shakespeare studies? Can we talk about Shakespeare's characters as if they were real people? How should we deal with false dichotomies, Shakespeare's perspectivism, contradiction and coexistence of two competing ideas at the same time? Did Shakespeare have a mind which could think otherwise?

Since the publication of literary theory masterpieces like Stephen Greenblatt's *Renaissance Self-Fashioning,* the conventional modes of Shakespearean criticism were overthrown. 'New historicism' and 'cultural materialism' have come to the forefront by becoming the dominant modes to study the great poet. Present-day literary theory has been shaped by the same institutional forces which shaped Elizabethan theatre. The plays of Shakespeare have been central to the growth of post-war literary and cultural criticism. The way early modern theatre overpowered the university, postmodern university now refashions the theatre recasting same disappearing subjects, ideological contradictions and imperialist illusions which it uncovers in Shakespeare.

We can easily locate the orderly juxtaposition of Shakespeare's works, especially his tragedies and comedies and the postmodern academy. The flowery vision of King Henry's theoric and his supreme power is in sharp contrast to the diseased perspective of Othello's arch-villain Iago who condemns his rival Cassio as a man of 'bookish theoric'. Both Iagoists and Henryists of every age, Elizabethan or contemporary, believe that literary theory belongs to an entirely different time and place from Shakespeare.

But when we critically analyze the plays of Shakespeare, we knowingly or unknowingly understand a theory. Some of the elements of contemporary literary theory we can decipher from Shakespeare's writings while others have mutated beyond recognition. The propounders of formalism, structuralism, deconstruction, psychoanalysis, Marxism, feminism state that Shakespeare is theoretical. Some of their readings are: Mikhail Bakhtin and carnivalesque in Shakespeare's festive drama; Roland Barthes on mythic speech in *Julius Caesar*; Jacques Derrida on the proper name and *Romeo and Juliet*; Sigmund Freud on the death in *King Lear*; Melanie Klein on envy in *Othello*; Jonathan Dollimore on perverse dynamic in *Othello*, and so on.

In the light of above discussion, my entry point to Shakespeare is whether in the light of present-day theorization we can revisit the question of 'appearance and reality' in Shakespeare's tragedies. There are multiple ways of understanding Shakespeare's plays but 'appearance and reality' continues to be very relevant.

Many theorists find that language is not a gateway to a pre-existing reality. There is always a web or structure within which the meaning reflected by the language becomes slippery and ambiguous. Shakespeare is always conscious about the ambiguity of language and the way it disturbs the social order. He has the genius and a ready wit to turn a word inside out and reflect undiscovered meaning. He enjoys word play and pun. He writes in a language which has a complex structure. Most of the words and phrases contain traces of others. The weird witches of *Macbeth* talk about the topsy-turvy order of the universe. Their forecasting about Macbeth and the state of Denmark is in the form of riddles which Macbeth understands much later. They assembled together amidst thunder, lightening and fog. Their speeches resemble a deadly rhyme. The language structure and style used by Shakespeare is a deliberate attempt to make everything look mysterious so that the style matches the appearance and the atmosphere. He calls them 'weird', which in old English meant 'fate', conveying that they were associated with Macbeth's fate which Macbeth is unable to control.

The Cyprus episode after the stormy journey in *Othello* is a good example. When Cassio greets Emilia and kisses her, Iago says:

> Sir, would she give you so much of her lips
> As of her tongue she oft bestows on me,
> You would have enough. (2.1.100-02)

Iago's words slip glibly between the literal kissing and the metaphorical speaking and scolding. He means to say that Emilia scolds him a lot and she criticizes him even when she is silent. In the same scene when Cassio takes Desdemona by her palm, Iago in an aside says:

> I will gyve thee in thine own courtship...well kissed and excellent courtesy. (2.1.168-73)

'Courtesy' along with 'courtship' may echo the 'manners' and 'breeding' by which Cassio justified kissing Emilia. The frequent using of the word 'honest' for Iago is misleading and ambiguous where there are many different meanings of the word. Othello's 'fair' creature suddenly becomes a 'whore' for him. Some critics say that the couple never consummated. Others say that they did and thus Othello had a feeling that he, as a black man has contaminated Desdemona's sexual and racial purity. Since her purity is destroyed, he calls her a whore and suspects her of having sex with Cassio as well. At another place Iago uses the language of war to describe his relationship with Othello—he'll 'show out a flag' as an indication of his loyalty.

Lynda E. Boose talks about the embroidery on the handkerchief of Desdemona which is most frequently referred to as the 'work'. Shakespeare has given form to a verbal echo with the help of a patterned growth of significance to reflect the symbolic meaning of red strawberry spots on the handkerchief. When a word is frequently repeated in various contexts at various places, with interconnected words and ideas, a faculty of discursive reasoning originates which explains and interprets the entire text. Iago uses this word in sexual context, Emilia as figuration, Othello and Cassio for embroidery. It became a 'bloody work' with Iago. It also becomes an incantation which Iago utters when Othello falls down in a trance.

The witty meaningful speeches of fool in *King Lear* where he makes Lear realize his folly are enough to acknowledge the role of language and structure. Apart from language, Shakespeare understands the power of sound and music. Who else than G. Wilson Knight could analyse the power of music and sound in *Othello*. The last speech of Othello is worth mentioning in this respect.

> When you shall these unlucky deeds relate,
> Speak of me as I am. Nothing extenuate,
> Nor set down aught in malice. (5.2.346-48)

Othello is anxious about his reputation after his death. He does not want others to misinterpret his motive and action. The power of music sufficiently conveys his last wish.

Regarding the ambiguities of literary language 'formalism' theory and its propounders suggest that by attending closely to them, an explanatory origin underlying their complexity could be found. In Shakespeare's tragedies also, it is the form that makes literary language so slippery. He too knows that in order to find an origin behind the text's multivocality or plurality of meaning, it is essential to understand its form. What a text says can never be separated from how the text says it. In this context, ambiguity, paradox and defamiliarization to make the familiar strange also become important.

Mikhail Bakhtin (1895-1975) states that carnival does not only mean the medieval festive holidays like May Day when hierarchy could be systematically inverted. Women would dress as men, children could mock the elderly people. It also projects a mass opinion of the universe which is in contrast to official cosmology of church and sovereign. The classical body image with its head ruling the lower parts is opposed to the laughing grotesque body of popular culture. In Shakespeare we can find examples of the carnivalesque. The strange equivocating witches in *Macbeth* seem to be the ambiguous foretellers who project a carnivalesque inversion and regeneration. We discover essential carnival elements in the organization of Shakespeare's other plays as well. He was indeed indebted to the festive popular culture of his day. This fact explains the clowning characters of his comedies as well as tragedies. In *King Lear*, *Hamlet*, and *Antony and Cleopatra* the upside down would visualize the carnival's power to fall and regenerate, to mock and reassert.

Othello can be read and interpreted as a carnivalesque text presenting a violent burlesque of marriage. Michael D. Bristol in his essay "Charivari and the Comedy of Abjection in Othello" (1990) talks about how the play's structure can be read as a parodic derangement of marriage as a social institution and the contrasting role of heterosexual desire within that institution. This desire is presented as an awkward mutual attraction between a fair woman and a clownish monster. The deployment of the stereotypical figure of a racially black man, comically portrayed by a white actor in black face heightens the carnivalesque element. Instead of the bride being represented by a man dressed as a woman, she is represented as hyper-feminine. Generally a transvestite plays the part of the woman and the bridegroom is played by a clownish character. This explains the fact that though the play is grouped with the tragedies, critics and theorists have witnessed the precarious balance of the play at the boundaries of farce. The racial otherness of Othello makes it a caricature. In *Hamlet* "The Play within the Play" has been presented as a public rebuke to the unseemly marriage of Claudius and Hamlet's mother.

The 'formalists' work with a word, line or a passage and deduce from it an array of meanings. They also work on a bigger canvas where instead of the small formal details, larger popular festive form is chosen. 'Structuralism' owes much to formalism as well as linguistic theory. It believes in a theoretical understanding of language as a system of differences. It says that every language consists of signs. The meanings of these signs are deduced through their variation from other similar or dissimilar signs, i.e. negatively.

Shakespeare's works employ a string of binary structuring devices like systematic hierarchical societies versus topsy-turvy world of carnival, courtly culture versus pastoral spaces, supernatural world of equivocating fiends versus calm, serene culture of a sophisticated society, upside down war culture versus the culture in which relations are based on mutual love and sympathy. He seems to be fascinated with signs and wants his readers to understand them as meaningful marks in the realm of text. A sign has an overt meaning and an entire range of implicit or alternate meanings that destabilise the seemingly dominant meaning. Plays like *Romeo and Juliet, Macbeth*, Othello and many others have abundance of signs and indications about how to construe and misconstrue them, how to decode them.

When Juliet asks 'Art thou not Romeo and a Montague?' (2.1.102), her question is meaningful both through its syntactical structure and in relation to the other absent signs from which any sign differs in conception. The two names used here are important "because of what they are not: 'Romeo' is not 'Paris' and 'Montague' is not 'Capulet'—the 'thou' addressed to Juliet is divided from her by the inter-familial tension of her city in which the difference between Montague and Capulet is not just merely semantic or conceptual but also deadly" (Jonathan Gill Harris 2010: 27). Roland Barthes talks about the semiology of 'Romanness' in Charles Mankiewicz's 1955 film adaptation of *Julius Caesar*. He tries to analyze the sub-sign of Portia's and Calpurnia's locks. Both are disordered. Both are as per the conventions of twentieth-century Hollywood, and at the same time, both reflect the timeless aura of natural sense. Another sign which is significant here is the 'sweat' sign which reflects 'to think in a different situation' as well as presents how the capitalist American culture converts thought into labour. The visions of dagger, bloody hands, ghost, etc. in *Macbeth* and other plays symbolically reflect the guilt of the wicked; the storm in *Julius Caesar* and *Othello* is a sign of the evil in the minds of the hostile or vicious people, while the plague is a sign which represents a process of undifferentiation or loss of individuality. The plague depicts the reversal of social order turning good into evil, maidens into immoral women, prosperity into misery, strength into happiness, and so on. Plays like *Macbeth* suggest the unstable terrain when it shows—'nothing isèk But what is not' (1.3.140-41).

Shakespeare's choice and arrangement of words is significant. When Othello describes that Desdemona fell in love with him while listening to his adventurous tales, he recalls that Desdemona said, "She wished.... That heaven had made her such a man" (1.3.161-62). This statement can be understood in many ways. It can be that Desdemona wishes heaven to have made such a man for her to marry. It can also be that Desdemona wishes heaven had made her a man instead of a woman. A girl like Desdemona may have a fondness for action and adventure. She even wishes to accompany Othello to Cyprus on his military expedition though she quietly unexpected passivity towards the end when she quietly allows Othello to kill her. In his essay "Othello and Colour Prejudice" (1967), G.K. Hunter talks about the dominant images that must have been present in the minds of Elizabethan audience. When the play opens, "We hear from men like us about a man not like us—of his 'Moorship', 'thick lips', 'black ram', 'Barbary horse'" (G.K. Hunter). We observe the sexual fear and disgust behind this racial prejudice. But when Othello appears it seems the appearance is not the reality. He is a great Christian or a Christian convert fighting against Turks, his own people to save Christendom. He is not a 'lascivious Moor' and chooses his military duties over his marital ones. He may be 'the devil' in appearance but 'honest' and 'fair' Iago is the sinner. Othello controls the reality of action and Iago controls only the appearance of talk. Shakespeare repeatedly seems to address the problem of thinking two logically contradictory things at once. Deconstructive readings of Shakespeare's text are done due to their language as well as their open-endedness. Both these aspects permit us to think of two different things at once. Whenever Shakespeare uses puns, they disclose the properties of language, reveal the social realities and highlight the instability of words in a topsy-turvy world.

'Psychoanalysis' understands desire in ways that radically destabilize gender and sexual identity. Shakespeare believes in the theory of desire and the confused identity induced by desire. Sigmund Freud (1856-1939) says that dreams communicate unconscious desires. He elaborates the relation of the unconscious to our dreams and daily behaviour and explains the psychic and sexual development of a man, right from his birth. The infant develops a strong sexual desire for his mother. The connection of this sexual longing, aggression (wish to kill father) and finally repression (prohibition or law) he names as 'Oedipus Complex'. We can discover these Oedipal overtones in sibling rivalries, professional rivalries, generation conflicts, political conflicts, caste and class conflicts and above all conflicts within oneself and so on. According to Freud a dream is a safety-valve to release the suppressed wishes, desires and emotions. From the realm of unconscious, they are shifted to conscious mind where they are not recognized or appreciated and thus go back to the dreams that is the unconscious mind in disguised form.

The unconscious feelings and desires are significant in case of both the author and the characters portrayed by him. The best known example to explain the difference between the appearance and reality with respect to Freudian psychoanalysis is both the play *Hamlet* and the character Hamlet. Hamlet's father's ghost appears to inform Hamlet about the real cause of the father's death. The ghost only confirms Hamlet's own suspicions regarding his father's death and his mother's hasty marriage with Claudius. Thus, what is already present in the subconscious of his mind finds expression in the form of ghost's revelation. His gesture and hurry in killing Polonius suggests that he is not a coward and that he has the courage and guts to avenge his father's death. But he procrastinates unnecessarily giving one reason or the other for doing so. His appearance demands us to believe what we see and read but something is yet to come out. Things can be interpreted in a different way. Freud perhaps is right when he says that Hamlet understands why he is unable to act. He can't kill Claudius for a crime which he himself wanted to commit. The Oedipus Complex in Hamlet which is the repressed sexual desire for his mother would have instigated him to kill his own father the way Claudius did. In the bedroom scene, he is unable to hide his intense awareness of Gertrude's sexuality. Freud goes far to the extent of connecting Shakespeare, the author with Hamlet but he could not discover Oedipal elements in him.

Claudius, the villain's inability to pray connects his behaviour with his unconscious mind which he knows is guilty. So, outwardly he seems to be calm and composed but all is not well within. The repressed feelings of his unconscious mind force him to behave abnormally during the staging of the "Play within the Play".

He is shocked, agitated and perturbed enabling Hamlet decipher the true significance of his gesture.

Freud also connects other plays of Shakespeare like *The Merchant of Venice* and *King Lear*, *Othello* and *Macbeth* with psychoanalytic theory. He employs it to decipher love, fate and death in *Macbeth*, *The Merchant of Venice* and *King Lear*. In *Macbeth* two separate individuals or criminals, i.e. Macbeth and Lady Macbeth can be represented as single psychical individual. In order to misguide and mislead others they smear the hands of the sleeping guards with Duncan's bloods to give the impression that they have killed him. They pretend to be shocked and agitated. Now, according to psychoanalytic theory when such unbelievable and unsatisfying reasons and justifications are given the language and the expressions of the persons reflect that there are concealed motives and emotions behind them. The vision of dagger again speaks in the accents of psychoanalysis.

In *The Merchant of Venice*, Bassanio definitely chooses right casket but the justification he gives for the same is not much convincing. We need to understand the psyche which contains hidden truths and reasons. Freud even says that Bassanio in choosing the right casket actually chooses the right woman out of the three. In Shakespeare's *King Lear* also, Lear makes a similar choice. Out of his three daughters, he rejects his youngest daughter Cordelia and believes that his other two daughters Goneril and Regan truly love him. Freud finds similarity between these plays. Bassanio chooses the casket with Portia's picture in it. A picture symbolises dumbness that is lack of life which is death. King Lear is happy to hear the extravagant professions of love from Regan and Goneril. The demonstration of false love or the pretension of love which means no love is preferred over true and silent love of Cordelia. This lack of love can be called as the death of love and feelings or death itself. In both the cases the character chooses death. Freud's psychoanalysis explains that the silence or dumbness (Bassanio's choice of silence picture and Lear's choice of false or no love) represents death. The tragic structure of *King Lear* perfectly carries forward this death symbolism and Lear finally suffers and dies. The comic structure of *The Merchant of Venice* distorts and reverses the meaning and the play ends happily. Bassanio is happily married to Portia and death remains far apart. The plays suggest how literary text can function by bringing repressed unconscious material to consciousness. Thus, there are different layers of meaning which are not evident from appearance or surface.

Othello is another tragedy by Shakespeare which is an obvious example of psychoanalysis and deals with the workings of the psyche. Othello connects his identity with Desdemona's sexuality. Mark Rose, in his essay "Othello's Occupation: Shakespeare and the Romance of Chivalry" talks about the 'Farewell' speech of Othello which he utters in Act 3, Sc. 3. Othello says good bye to his happiness, peace and satisfaction which evokes the pastoral ideal. The imagery of 'big wars' and 'plumed troops' evokes the military ideal. The repetition of the word 'Farewell' makes the speech coherent and persuasive and adds to the perception of a military procession which passes before Othello when he is saying goodbye to the squadrons in the parade. The squadrons represent the pleasures of his life. The repetition of the word also unifies the speech as well as the contradictory pastoral and military imagery. Othello banishes himself from the perfected world or heaven of absolute being at the mere suspicion of his wife's infidelity. His 'occupation as a soldier' is ruined and his real identity lost when the illusory suspicion goes deep inside him.

At some places the conscious and the unconscious match. T.S. Eliot may not be very convincing when he says that Othello is "cheering himself up" in his last speech when he tries to escape reality. He stops thinking about Desdemona, the source of his life and identity and only thinks about his reputation. Eliot calls this "bovarysme" which means the human desire to see things as they are not. Othello does that consciously as well as unconsciously.

Keogh opines that in the days of Sophocles "the mother city had become a goddess, and her children were told to become her lovers" (Keogh, 'O City, City': 109). He draws "an analogy with *Coriolanus* by arguing that when Coriolanus is on the point of attacking his mother-city Rome, his wife and his mother... manage to dissuade him. The metropolis is a sacred personage; any attack on her, likely to involve rape and pillage, was thought to invoke the same taboos as forbad incest" (Keogh, 'O City, City': 112). Coriolanus refrains from attacking and destroying Rome. His relationship with his mother, Volumnia, seems incestuous enough to make him a very Oedipal figure. He cannot take any decision or action without taking his mother's consent and Volumnia, very craftily takes all credit for his heroic and brave deeds by insisting, 'They valiantness was mine, thou suck'st it from me' (1.3.2-3). Her 'attentions betray an erotic interest that even her rigid authority can't conceal; in giving unwanted advice to Coriolanus' wife, Volumnia puts herself in her daughter-in-law's place with alarming alacrity, speculating, 'If my son were my husband' (Shakespeare, *Coriolanus* 1.3.2-3) (Bradley W. Buchanan 2010). The desire of Coriolanus to murder his own people serves as an 'objective correlative' to the Oedipal desires as seen by Freud. When Coriolanus expresses his wish to remake humanity in his own image, 'That would depopulate the city andèk Be every man himself' (3.1.264-65) he reminds us of Oedipus' solution to the riddle of the Sphinx (whereby all beings are defined, as he is, by their feet).

Virginia Woolf in her essay "Shakespeare's Sister" (1929) seems to challenge the notion of literary work as a self-contained artifact detached from the author and the society in which it is written. No woman could achieve what Shakespeare achieved during a favourable and flowering literary age. The reason given by her is philosophically materialist. She believes that one's being does not determine one's material conditions but vice versa is true. Karl Marx also drew on these lines. Woolf says that Shakespeare's plays may give the illusion of being free works of individual genius but they actually originate from material conditions that divide men and women on the basis of class and gender. Women's material lot militates against their creativity. Almost a contradictory view is explained by Helene Cixous when she says that feminine creativity is grounded in her material lot or her body: "Woman must write her body" (Cixous 1986: 84). She does not accept the traditional patriarchal writing of male and female bodies. Shakespeare's scenes are scenes of endless becoming. A man or a boy actor turns into a woman and then again to a man. In this way the writing of the body is performed in Shakespeare. She praises the gender fluidity in *Romeo and Juliet* where the two lovers reject their patriarchal identities. In *Antony and Cleopatra*, there is, "The lusty queen, to whom everything is becoming—scolding, laughing, crying—at every instant another face, at each breath a passion, flesh struggling with a desire for more love, more life, more pleasure, at every moment, the queen with ten tongues; she spoke them all" (Cixous 1986: 123). Cleopatra is criticized for her lack of a singular identity. Cixous also valourises Antony who loves Cleopatra truly and also loves the feminine within himself. He is happy in his darling's sexual games in which she dresses him up in her 'tires and mantles' and herself wears his sword 'Philippan'. In this reversal, the seemingly opposites cross over and find a common ground. Talking about Ophelia's relative marginality in *Hamlet* the American feminist literary critic Elaine Showalter opines, "Ophelia does have a story of her own that feminist criticism can tell; it is neither her life story, nor her love story, nor Lacan's story, but rather the history of her representation" (Showalter 1994: 223). Hamlet's madness, whether it is real or feigned, is not motiveless but Ophelia's madness is seen as entirely feminine. It is analyzed as love melancholy or hysteria. Shakespeare's contemporary society believed that a woman's womb needed to be sexually fed, otherwise it would detach itself, roam through the body, reach brain finally to feed on it, leading to hysteria. This type of criticism continued till nineteenth century. In early twentieth century it was argued that her madness was caused by her mistreatment through the patriarchal forces of Hamlet and Polonius. One is not born a woman but becomes one. Woolf seems to highlight her view that a text is not free-standing. It is chained to the society—both contemporary as well as the ever changing society in which it is reproduced. The meaning of 'woman' also changes, so the word cannot be regarded as a signifier with a fixed signified.

Moving from 'feminist criticism' to 'Marxist criticism' it can be said that Karl Marx analysed the effects of industrial capitalism on society and laid the foundations for a materialist literary criticism which says that an author's social class and its outlook, morals and values have a lot to do with what he writes.

Material conditions shape culture and to a great extent culture shapes literature. Marx's pioneering sketches of materialist literary criticism are guided by the suggestion that certain system of social and economic organization produces certain types of literature. He interprets ancient Greek literature and Shakespeare's drama in relation to their societies' different means of material production.

Theories like 'Marxism', 'new historicism', 'cultural materialism', 'postcolonial theory' analyse a text in the light of cultural and historical background. The Marxist study of Shakespeare deals with the inner contradictions of feudalism. The dramatist has a keen eye on the human conflicts originated by declining feudalism.

There are frequent references to society's transition from feudalism to capitalism in Shakespeare though his theorisation of social transition differs according to genre as well as the chronology of his works. While on one hand *The Merchant of Venice* depicts a fruitful marriage between old feudal wealth of Portia and Bassanio's (or Antonio's) new merchant capital, *Macbeth* depicts declining feudalism. *King Lear* portrays disastrous end of old feudal values at the hands of selfish individualism of Edmund, the Bastard. *Othello* vividly depicts Desdemona as her father's property or possession which he is unwilling to transfer except to his own people. Othello also tries to possess her as his wealth only. Desdemona becomes a property—First in the hands of her father Brabantio who is scared of losing her and then with Othello who wants to possess her entirely. Property always fears theft and so when Iago and Roderigo rouse sleeping Brabantio they shout "Thieves, thieves, thieves!" They mean to say that Othello has stolen her from Brabantio. Here, Iago plays on fear of miscegenation that is interracial sex or marriage. He says that an 'old black ram' that is Othello, is 'tupping' his 'white ewe' which is Desdemona. Shakespeare's word play is important here. Ewe is a lamb; thus, Iago suggests that Desdemona's white skin makes her morally pure and her lamblike purity is being spoiled by a black man (ram). The deliberate use of animal metaphor is remarkable. He also refers to the Elizabethan view that black men have an animal like hyper-sexuality.

At another point in the play Othello talks about sex as—a fruit to enjoy, something which profits both men and women. The use of financial metaphors 'purchase' and 'profits' seems a bit strange and out of the place. If Othello already had this materialistic view about marriage and sex before anything bad happens, he leaves enough scope for suspicion and jealousy to creep in. His actual state of mind is difficult to judge. Taking a clue from Dick Hebdige's *Subculture: The Meaning of Style* (1979), the relationship of Desdemona and Emilia, the two female characters of the play, can be demonstrated as one of the very first expressions of 'subculture'. Their gossips and interaction with each other can be understood as a way of style or culture within a culture to expose the hollowness and the evils of the Renaissance patriarchal order. The emergence of resistance against the power of the Western male hegemonic discourse can also be looked at.

Elizabethan women were thought of as expressions of objects of male desire. A parallel reading of other literary and non-literary texts such as various conduct books, law books and manuals, which we can call a 'new historic' approach, tells us that all these books preached women to pay close attention to the office and duties of a wife. Her status as a human being was subjugated by her status as a devoted and dutiful daughter and wife. Wedding in *Othello* is like Levi-Strauss' description—a relationship between two groups of men and not between a man and a woman. In this process women become a kind of illustration of the 'male economy of desire' to be exchanged between men. When Desdemona expresses her view to be subjected to the 'utmost pleasure' of her lord, a culture can be visualized wherein male homosexuality can be described as a code which governs the socio-cultural order while heterosexuality assigns roles in the economy. Here, homosexuality is a term with different connotations. It does not represent sex between two men but "deprecates the feminine and invests the masculine with sexual desire accompanied by fear, guilt and loathing of female sexuality" (Boose: 28). Not only Desdemona but all the women of the play are "the fair papers on which the men of the play write 'whore'" (Boose: 38). Even a minor figure like Roderigo believes that Desdemona can be available for sexual purchase if he has gold and jewels enough. She is always described and circumscribed in a language which talks of her as an object or a commodity. The use of language by the senators to 'use Desdemona well' gives an indication to her possessor that she is an object to be possessed and enjoyed.

Critics like Kenneth Burke have always read Act 4, Sc. 3 as an example of foreboding representing Desdemona as 'doubly frail' but on 'deconstruction' the same scene can be read as a style or culture or power to question the patriarchal discourse. Desdemona and Emilia form a subculture by coming together and speaking to one another without the laws of the 'market' whose 'goods' or 'commodities' they are. They represent 'female homosexuality' which resists 'male homosexuality'. They form a 'community' of women together with the women of the past that is Desdemona's mother and her maid, Barbary. Their seemingly idle chatter, when Desdemona also sings the willow song, reveals the misogynist discourse embedded in the structure of whole Venetian society or the broader structure of Renaissance society.

By subculture, Dick Hebdige implies "style as a form of refusal" in a different perspective. But this refusal can be seen in Desdemona also. She challenges the accepted values of the dominant culture. Her frequency matches with another exchangeable commodity, Emilia. In a language of gossips, songs and narratives they destabilise the male order from within. By being a part of a sympathetic confederate, they seriously threaten and expose the fissures in patriarchy. Traditional criticism regards willow scene as 'pity scene' exposing the vulnerability and frailty and suppressed voice of women with pathos, but this scene is truly a scene where voice of women is heard. This is a space beyond the symbolic order of men which is unrestrained and uncontrolled by men. The performance history of Othello tells us how cleverly this scene has been consistently reduced or removed from performances. This scene is a subcultural response to a dominant culture.

When Desdemona sings 'Let nobody blame him, his scorn I approveèk Nay, that's not next' (4.3.52-53). She in a sub-cultural gesture, adopts a 'self'. The traditional ballad may represent passive suffering of unrequited love, but Desdemona, probably, is affirming her own power of love. The song depicts male unfaithfulness which results in female wantonness. In the end, this subculture is victorious as Emilia finds the voice to speak the truth by exposing her husband and rebuking Othello for his objectification of women.

About Shakespeare's *Timon of Athens*, Marx says that the play 'excellently depicts the real nature of money' (Marx 1975: 103). Timon has to abandon his luxurious life. He goes to the wilderness and after some time discovers some gold buried in the ground. He starts thinking about the evils of money:

> Thus much of this will make black white, foul fair,
> Wrong right, base noble, old young, coward valiant.
> (4.3.1691-92)

He says that money transforms people to become their opposites based on their capacity to buy things. Thus there is a perversion of the natural order of man and things. Man exercises full authority over an object when he possesses or uses it directly but he transfers his authority to the inanimate object that is 'gold' when he thinks that this 'gold' will buy him everything. The 'gold' is transformed into an authority with creative power. That is why Timon assigns active verbs to gold like 'will make', 'will break'. In Act 4, Sc. 3, he calls money 'a whore' as well a 'visible god'. The paradox is interesting. If a whore, money forces a confusion of the 'false' for the 'true' (a moneyed customer or a true lover) unlike when it is a visible god. Marx also is satisfied with the language and the tone used by Shakespeare in this play. According to his analysis, the upside down world of Timon truly matches with the topsy-turvy materialistic world of capitalistic society where black becomes white, foul becomes fair, wrong becomes right, virtue turns into vice, hate into love, folly into wisdom and vice versa, due to money power. The money or the commodity overpowers and dominates man by inverting the subject–object relation. Capitalism cherishes the idea that a commodity's exchange value is present in the commodity itself and not in the human labour associated with it. Thus, the relationship between the people who produce and exchange the goods gives place to a relationship between the goods produced and exchanged.

The Marxist reading of the play *Coriolanus* explains the contradictions and hidden elements in the mutiny between hungry Roman plebeians and the upper class patricians. In the new capitalist theatres this mutiny between the two classes was presented largely from the perspective of patricians. The revolt of plebeians was seen as a proof of their unreliability. The only remarkable thing in the scene was the heroic stature of the patrician warrior Marcius. A close reading of the play informs us that the play does not deal much with social totality. It talks more about the local conflicts hidden behind the bigger looking social issue. From the surface the plebeians seem to be a homogeneous united group in rebellion with Patricians, but there are contradictions and disputes within. Some of the other contradictions are—"the unrest of the starving plebeians plus the war against their neighbours the Volscians; the plebeians' hatred for Marcius, the people's enemy-plus his patriotism; the creation of the People's Tribune—plus Marcius's appointment to a leading role in the war" (Brecht 1992: 255).

In some other plays like *Hamlet*, *Othello*, *King Lear*, and *Macbeth* the dramatic techniques like—play within a play, presence of clown or fool, cross-dressing, boy actors playing the part of women defamiliarise our understanding of what is real or natural. In the process, the underlying or hidden social contradictions are revealed. This 'alienation-effect' as specified by Bertolt Brecht, a German playwright (1898-1956) exposes the clash between medieval feudalism and a rising code of individualistic upward mobility. Brecht also employs this concept to explain Hamlet's inability to avenge his father's death by killing Claudius.

'Postcolonial criticism' rejects the universalism of a work propounding that in the process of universalism the Western-centred or European-centred norms are promoted and all others are marginalised. It is against the belief in the superiority of everything that is Western and inferiority of everything that is not. There are frequent references to Europe's rising power in Shakespeare in the form of Antonio's fortune depending on his trade with 'the Indies' and 'Mexico' (I.3.16-17) in *The Merchant of Venice*. Troilus believes Cressida to be a pearl in 'India' and himself as a merchant pining for this gem, and so on. Wole Soyinka, in his essay "Shakespeare the Living Dramatist" (1983) opines that Shakespeare has portrayed something authentic about Egypt, apart from its scenery, pyramids and river Nile. *Antony and Cleopatra* can be read as an allegory of the Egyptian struggle for independence from the British Empire with Cleopatra presented as a lady torn between love for her nation and love for Antony. In his famous tragedy *Othello,* Shakespeare has depicted Orient and Islam and outsiders having a particular role to play inside Europe. Like many other plays, Shakespeare uses 'Orient' as a term for a homogeneously exotic East presented in opposition to Europe. In a sense, Postcolonial theory disorients our understanding of Shakespeare's written lines. This theory discovers mixed genealogies which do not merely reproduce the authority of England or Europe.

Almost all the literary theories reflect that Shakespeare's plays do not belong to a singular place. They materialise diverse orientations and disorientations. They transform and reestablish Shakespeare—leading his texts in new directions.

Ritu Saluja

1
Macbeth

Out of the four major tragedies written by Shakespeare *Macbeth* is the shortest, darkest and most powerful tragedy. It is most commonly dated 1606 and was most likely written during the reign of James I. Shakespeare found the story of Macbeth in the book *Chronicles of England, Scotland and Ireland* by Raphael Holinshed. For the part of the play dealing with the supernatural, he took hints from Reginald Scot's *Discourse of Witchcraft* (1597). Shakespeare has deviated from his sources according to dramatic necessity, and the deviations are a measure of his genius.

Macbeth is a complex work of art, and there are number of themes and ideas in it like 'order-disorder-order', 'appearance versus reality', 'exploration of evil in its different manifestations', 'the inevitability of retribution which follows close on evil doing', 'the opposition of life and death forces', 'personal aspiration and political ambition', 'the seductive and destructive possibilities of power', 'ingratitude', etc.

Revisiting Shakespeare in a Freudian way is like entering into a new realm of discovering something really well-known but mysteriously intriguing. Freud makes the character study much complex than it really is and his valuable insight into Shakespeare's characters is praiseworthy. Shakespeare is a true genius in searching the human mind and dramatizing it and

Freud is an expert at mapping it out. He employs the science of psychoanalysis to explain the text in terms of forces and energies to reproduce in the internal world the laws which govern the external world. Harold Bloom rightly says, "What we think of as Freudian psychology is really a Shakespearean invention... Freud is merely codifying it" (Bloom 1991).

Freud in the last years of his life confessed that throughout his life he made attempts to penetrate king Macbeth. He says that Macbeth and Lady Macbeth are actually a single personality. Shakespeare sometimes splits a character into two personages. The elements of tension and fear which figure out in Macbeth after the first murder ultimately surface in Lady Macbeth.

> It is he who has the hallucination of the dagger before the crime; but it is she who afterwards falls ill of a mental disorder. It is he who after the murder hears the cry in the house: "Sleep no more! Macbeth does murder sleep..." and so "Macbeth shall sleep no more", but we never hear that he slept no more, while the Queen, as we see, rises from her bed and, talking in her sleep, betrays her guilt.... Thus what he fears in his pangs of conscience is fulfilled in her.... Together they exhaust the possibilities of reaction to the crime, like two disunited parts of a single psychical individuality. (Freud 1916: 324)

In his clinical study related to mental aberrations and personality disorder problems Freud draws freely on Macbeth. He propounds a strange proposition that a person occasionally falls sick when a deep-rooted and long-cherished desire comes to fulfillment. This he calls 'wrecked by success'. He further says that an example of one wrecked by success is the case of Lady Macbeth. She collapses on achieving success. Against the background of Jacobian Age when James succeeded to the throne of virginal childless Queen Elizabeth Freud, sees an important suggestion of childlessness. "It would be a perfect example of poetic justice...if Macbeth could not become a father because he had robbed children of their father (in Banquo's case) and a father of his children (in Macduff's case), and if Lady Macbeth suffered the unsexing she had demanded of the spirits of murder...

the transformation of her callousness into penitence, could be explained directly as a reaction to her childlessness..." (Freud 1916: 321). Freud could not come to any conclusion with regards to questions about the accuracy of Shakespeare's depiction of their motivation and the psychic breakdown of Lady Macbeth but this indeed is one way of interpreting the characters.

Freud propounds that dreams express desire and the inner truth of the subject. Michel Foucault was a critic of Freud's psychoanalysis and 'repressive hypothesis'. According to Foucault dreams are not so much expressions of inner truths as mediations of a world organized in time as well as space. In this sense dreams are not simply the repressed desires but are also revelatory premonitions, directed towards a future shared by the dreamer and his world. The theorist historicizes dreams and madness in Macbeth. He discovers the real meaning of dreams in their existential aspect. He examines how Macbeth is said to murder sleep. If sleep relieves us of the agonies of our worldly existence, dreams reacquaint us with those agonies. Dreams make sleep impossible by waking it to the light of death. In case of Macbeth, dream murders his sleep and confronts him with death. This is a universal condition of existence (existentialism). A text speaks through many different voices. Outwardly *Macbeth* appears to be a play which dramatizes the disastrous, moral, psychological, social and political consequences produced when villainy and unnatural ways are used to fulfill the lust for power and wealth but it is very difficult to discover if something is really fair or foul. They are actually mixed up. Again and again it is stressed that things are not what they appear to be. Not only the people, but the predictions and the psyche seem to be playing tricks. False face does again and again hide the truth that lies in the heart. One cannot judge a person by his appearance only because appearances are deceptive. In order to understand a person correctly one has to understand his untold tale. In this play, I will try to bring to light the difference between appearance and reality through Witches, Macbeth, Lady Macbeth, Banquo, Macduff, Malcom and other characters. In this play we find a lot of situations through which this particular aspect is clearly reflected.

Atmosphere may be defined as the background against which the action of a play takes place. Like every Shakespearean tragedy, Macbeth has a special atmosphere of its own. In the opening scene of the play, the words of the Witches—

> Fair is foul, and foul is fair:
> Hover through the fog and filthy air. (1.1.10-11)

strike the keynote of the atmosphere of the play. Fair becomes foul and foul becomes fair in this play of evil, crime and villainy. Nature is foul from the beginning to the end and the foul in nature closely corresponds to the foul or evil in the soul of the hero. Macbeth, the hero of the play commits the foul deeds and it seems as if the nature is in harmony with his guilt and villainy. The wickedness or blackness in Macbeth and Lady Macbeth corresponds with the blackness of the atmosphere. The nature is feverish, full of evil omens as if in harmony with human guilt and the malice of the supernatural. The supernatural Witches, Ghost and the strange happenings in nature, the darkness of the night and the evil in Macbeth all combine together to create the general effect.

The words of the Witches reverse the natural order of things. The words reflect that the tragedy takes place in a demoralized atmosphere, where the moral values of humanity are allowed to be upset and perverted. All around there is a confusion of values and elements. The wild waste, the thunder and lightning, the mewing of cats, the croaking of toads, the ugly forms of the Witches and the strange words spoken by them—all these sights and sounds depict a state of confusion in Scotland where honest and reliable generals murder their kings and turn their houses into butchering places. 'Fair is foul and foul is fair' is the satanic principle of 'evil be thou my good'. In reality, this doctrine of Witches is self-deceiving because 'foul' is not 'fair'. It only appears to be fair. The first half of their utterance seems to be true because what should have been fair that is 'kingship' becomes foul and polluted by the means by which it is obtained. The Witches promise Macbeth of things that do sound fair. He receives kingship but feels that he has sold his soul, his eternal jewel for something that comes out to be worthless. These words of the Witches are symbolic of the treachery of Macbeth and the unnatural behaviour he adopts after the murder of King Duncan. The words denote that appearances are not to be trusted. The fair words of loyalty spoken by Macbeth and Lady Macbeth hide the foulness of their hearts. These words also suggest that human nature is a mixture of evil and good. The virtuous hero has weaknesses and a vicious villain has a good conscience. The best of us have some bad traits and the worst of us have some good traits.

The words of Witches have profound influence on Macbeth. This is seen in the fact that on his very first appearance on the stage, he closely echoes their words when he says:

> So foul and fair a day I have not seen. (1.3.38)

The Witches tempt him and take him away from goodness. He hears them voice the desires of his heart. His mind moves along the route they indicate.

It's too late that he realizes that the Witches have their own purposes into which men fit and which men can serve. Macbeth wishes them say what is in his own mind. He is afraid to acknowledge it as his own. The Witches utter riddles, which Macbeth in his weakness interprets in his own apparent interest. Actually, he is deceived not by the Witches but by his own wrong interpretations of their riddles. A belief in the existence of the supernatural—ghosts, fairies, Witches, etc. is found in all ages and times. So it was in Shakespearean age. Shakespeare also introduces supernatural in his plays. The supernatural in Macbeth is of two kinds—the Witches and the Ghost of Banquo. The Witches in their appearance and in their supernatural powers confirm the popular conception about them. In the present play, the fascination of the Witches lies in a combination of two different attitudes about them—the superstitious and the sceptical. They are real and vivid according to the popular belief, but there are also suggestions that they are the products of excited imagination, and so hallucinatory in nature. We can't deny the fact that the Witches are real beings. They are objective creatures of popular superstition. They are not merely the illusion of the hero. That is why Banquo is also able to see them. Had they been merely the illusion of Macbeth, they would have been visible only to Macbeth.

Though the Witches are objective and real, they have a deeper significance as well. They are also the symbolic representation of evil in the heart of Macbeth. He startles on hearing their words and this clearly reflects the close affinity between their prophecy and his own consciousness. He is tempted by them only because the temptation was already within his soul. Banquo is not tempted because he has no temptation within his soul. He does not believe in their words to the extent of acting upon them. He believes that there are powers of evil which deceive people with a fair appearance but whose inward purposes are dark and destructive. He thinks that the Witches represent those evil spirits who play a trick upon people with a half guilty soul harbouring crimes and evil thoughts. They at first win the confidence of a person by fulfilling some trivial desires and wishes of his heart, and then tempt him to do some evil which leads to his damnation. He believes that the Witches are using the thaneship of Cawdor as a bait to catch the soul of Macbeth for disastrous deeds. As the play proceeds, we realize that Banquo is absolutely correct in judging the character of Witches.

The words of Hecate truly describe their evil purposes in luring Macbeth to his Doom—

> And that, distill'd by magic sleights,
> Shall raise such artificial sprites
> As by the strength of their illusion,
> Shall draw him on to his confusion.
> He shall spurn fate, scorn death, and bear
> His hopes 'bove wisdom, grace, and fear;
> And you all know security
> Is mortals' chiefest enemy. (3.5.26-33)

Banquo dismisses them with indifference. He even doubts the existence of Witches which sometimes appear to be living creatures while another time seem to be shadowy figures. The reversal of moral order and values is apparent in their own deformity. They have very unnatural appearance. They should be women but their beards deny it. "Finally, they are unnatural in the most obvious, physical sense, being neither male nor female, and therefore, they symbolize how diseased the universe is in Macbeth, and how unnatural are the actions that will take place in the play" (Martin Stephen and Philip Franks 1984: 63). Banquo doubts their sex. He is unable to decide whether they are men or women.

Unlike the Witches, the Ghost of Banquo is entirely hallucinatory in character. It is an externalization of Macbeth's guilt and fear of discovery, invisible to others but a horrible reality to Macbeth himself. It acts as an instrument of justice and punishment. Its role is either to expose murder or to rouse people to avenge the murder. Macbeth's guilty imagination creates it. It is just like the dagger he sees before the murder of Duncan. That is why none else except him sees the ghost. He himself later on regards him as a shadow—

> Hence, horrible shadow !
> Unreal mockery, hence ! (3.4.106 07)

The play is full of false appearances. Shakespeare presents a world of false values in which Macbeth is guided by false apparitions and hallucinations. His moral sense becomes confused like his physical senses when he cannot distinguish the real from the unreal dagger. He follows unreality when the unreal dagger or the illusion of dagger directs him towards the murder. After he commits the murder, Lady Macbeth tries to console him with the illusory resemblance between the sleeping and the dead. She says that there is no difference between a sleeping person and a dead person. So, Macbeth should not be terrified by seeing the dead body of Duncan. But after a short while Macduff calls them to see death itself, the real death of the king. After murdering Duncan, Macbeth also hears illusory voice saying that he cannot sleep any more for he has murdered the sleeping King.

The character of Macbeth is very controversial. There are two opposite views about him which make him both a hero and a villain. Actually, he is both a hero and a villain. Shakespeare has made a hero out of a villain and a villain out of a hero. Many critics like Caroline Spurgeon support the view that perhaps Shakespeare himself wished to degrade Macbeth by making him wear ill fitted garments. His robes seem either too big like his mighty ambition or too small like his weak character wholly unsuited for the newly acquired kingship. Macbeth appears to have imperial magnificence, but in reality he is a 'dwarfish thief in a giant's robe'. Banquo truly comments that the new honour that is the title of Thane of Cawdor comes upon him like strange garments. At the end Caithness sees him as a man making futile efforts to fasten a large garment on him with too small a belt. He wants to convey the idea that human nature is a mixture of good and evil.

That Macbeth is a noble and gifted man worthy of honour is made clear before he falls a victim to evil powers. He is presented to us as a brave warrior and an able General. The king calls him 'a peerless kinsman' and other characters in the play call him noble and honourable. He has a number of good qualities of head and heart for which he is honoured and loved by all. After reading the play we realize that the state, exposed to the rebellion and invasion of traitors and enemies, needs a ruler of Macbeth's caliber—strong, brave and irresistible. Such type of qualities we find in Macbeth when we meet him for the first time in the play, seen from without and observed by unbiased eyes. But when we see his outlook on life, we find that his inner life is distinguished from his outer life. In support of this view we may take up the words of his own wife, one who knows him best. In order to judge his character correctly, we will have to keep in mind Lady Macbeth's comment about him when he communicates to her his meeting with the weird sisters. She says:

> Yet do I fear thy nature;
> It's too full of the milk of human kindness
> To catch the nearest way, Thou would be great;
> Art not without ambition but without
> The illness should attend it. What thou wouldst highly
> That wouldst thou holily; wouldst not play false,
> And yet wouldst wrongly win. (1.5.13-19)

When we closely analyze his character in the light of Lady Macbeth's statement, we find that Macbeth hesitates from doing an unnatural act. There is no predisposition of crime in him. He is good in every respect. He is to be considered a hero, not a villain. But what he does and what he is, happens to be two opposite things. And here lies the tragedy. Despite his being a brave, heroic soldier, Macbeth is weak of will and is easily carried away by the suggestions of others. He even acts against his own better judgment. He is never unaware of the futility and enormity of the crime he commits. The brave soldier becomes a murderer, usurper and tyrant because of one evil in him that he is over ambitious. He is ambitious to have the kingship not only for his own self, but also for his progeny. It is this evil in him that transforms him from a hero to a murderer. Edward Dowden rightly says—"He has aptitude for goodness and aptitude for crime" (Dowden 1970: 250).

Macbeth's goodness is overshadowed by his over-ambitious nature, and his wife Lady Macbeth helps him in the process. Lady Macbeth is a woman of iron will and determination and equally ambitious like him. It is she who spurs him to commit the crime. She calls her husband coward and foolish when she sees his repulsions before and after Duncan's murder. His remarkable success as a warrior, his consciousness of his own powers, Duncan's declaration of Malcom as his successor and above all the prophecy of the Witches act as spurs leading him towards his doom. Ambition becomes so strong in him that it suppresses all other voices in him. This evil in him becomes stronger and stronger with every advance he makes in his bloody career. The first thought that comes to him after hearing the words of the Witches is one of extreme horror at murder as a means to achieve his ambition. He leaves the whole business to chance and fate. He says:

> If chance will have me King,
> Why, chance may crown me. (1.3.143-44)

He shrinks and hesitates at the mere thought of the murder. Left to himself, he would never have done it. He begins to think whether the Witches are good and real or evil and imaginary. The imaginary scene of murder which he is now thinking or the very idea of murder overpowers his thoughts and makes him confused. The result is that he is no longer his real self. For him the facts have no reality and imaginary things are real—

> My thought, whose murder yet is but fantastical,
> Shakes so my single state of man

That function is smother'd in surmise,
And nothing is but what is not. (1.3.138-41)

But the idea that he has already become the Thane of Cawdor comforts him. He considers the Witches as the truth telling agents of his future greatness. He fails to judge what is real and what is imaginary. His deed of murder is done in a situation over which he has no control. He is a man obsessed and possessed by powers beyond his control. Once Macbeth plants his foot into the mud of bloody crime, there is no escape from it. He sinks deeper and deeper into it and could not find the way out of it. He achieves his aim by committing his first crime and now he is ready to do anything to secure the crown. His behavior, before and after the murder, shows the stirrings of his conscience which he cannot help facing, being what he is. He pretends to ignore the consequences of his deed in the life to come. But it is clearly seen that he is deeply stirred by the horror of what he does. He says that he is only concerned with the present consequences of his crime in this world. But this is not true. He is spiritually and morally alive to the horror of his crime and it is his imagination which opens for him the gates of conscience. Even when he commits the senseless murder of the innocent wife and children of Macduff, he is not free from his guilty conscience. He turns his back from Macduff in the last scene and is unwilling to face and fight him. He says—

....my soul is too much charged
With blood of thine already. (5.8.5-6)

These words reveal the most pathetic cry of Macbeth's anguished soul. In the end, he realizes that he has destroyed himself because of his overpowering ambition. Besides vaulting ambition, he has poetic imagination. It is pictorial and makes him have hallucinations. It makes him see the dagger and the ghost of Banquo. It forces upon him the fatal consequences of the murder. It is his imagination which makes him hear the voice of his conscience that he would not sleep any more for he has murdered the sleep or the sleeping king. His imagination is the expression of all that is good in him. Had he listened to it his end would have been different. When his imagination is active, he acts badly and his face betrays his guilt. When it is asleep, he is firm and self-controlled. Thus, despite his villainy and brutality, we find that he is an essentially noble character who acts against his nature under the influence of many factors.

When we discuss the good qualities of Macbeth, we do not approve his deeds. Shakespeare does not want us to compromise with evil and to take the side of the criminal. Whatever may be the factors that push Macbeth to do the evil, he certainly commits the most horrible crime. His loyalty to King Duncan is deceptive. He professes loyalty to the king and afterwards murders him for his selfish motives. He outwardly appears to be faithful towards the King but is treacherous towards him inwardly. This hypocritical attitude leads him to commit crime which leads to the tragedy. He seems to be very honest towards Duncan when he says that he and his wife would be very happy to welcome Duncan in their castle. But in the very next speech we see the germs of evil in him when he says—

Stars, hide your fires;
Let not light see my black and deep desires. (1.4.50-51)

When he is prepared for the murder of King Duncan he himself says to his wife—

I am settled, and bend up
Each corporal agent to this terrible feat.
Away, and mock the time with fairest show;
False face must hide what the false heart doth know. (1.7.79-82)

In these words he declares that now he is ready to do the deed. He says that he will act the part of a conscious hypocrite suggesting how a man may smile and be a villain. He will cover the treachery of his heart by a pretended innocent face. He will put on smiling appearance to deceive others. In one of his speeches, he also suggests the idea of sprinkling some blood upon the sleeping guard in order to establish that the guards have murdered the king—

Will it not be receiv'd,
When we have mark'd with blood those sleepy two
Of his own chamber, and us'd their very daggers,
That they have done't? (1.7.74-77)

The murder of Duncan is done under the illusion of safety, security and impunity. After murdering Duncan Macbeth shows as if he knows nothing about the murder. He says that life is meaningless to him because Duncan is dead. The doubleness of his character is clearly seen. On one hand, he is playing the part of an innocent, horrified host who is shocked at the murder of his royal guest. On the other hand, he is giving expression to a sense of real remorse at his own guilt. Life is really meaningless for him not because Duncan is dead but because his guilty conscience has crushed its joy. Macbeth kills the bodyguards of Duncan and tries to justify his act by saying that he did so out of his love and loyalty for the king. It seemed to him that the grooms had murdered their King because their hands and faces were found to be bloody. Here Macbeth thinks that he is covering up his guilt by acting the part of an angry avenger of his dead king. But he forgets that he is overacting his part. No one, in fact, is deceived by his false speech. He forgets that no murderers would keep their bloody daggers near them and then quietly go to sleep. His words could not convince others. Ironically, he expresses his own guilt in an effort to hide it. Here, Shakespeare suggests that the pretension of being innocent cannot hide the guilt of a person. Somehow it comes to the surface. He puts on fair appearance to hide his treachery. He again and again refers to the murderer's need for fair appearance. The false appearance he assumes temporarily becomes a settled practice later on. By the time he is planning to murder Banquo it has become a burden for him. He says—

> Unsafe the while, that we
> Must lave our honours in these flattering streams.
> And make our faces vizards to our hearts.
> Disguising what they are. (3.2.32-35)

A little before the banquet given by him, Macbeth urges his wife to flatter Banquo because that is the need of the hour. Inwardly, Macbeth is full of hatred for Banquo. But outwardly, he appears to be friendly towards Banquo, and advises his wife to pay particular attention to Banquo at the feast. He says that in order to keep ourselves free from suspicion, we have to hide our feelings towards those whom we hate under a mask of outward respect and friendship. In order to achieve his aim, he even removes his best friend from his way. He fills the ears of the murderers against Banquo. He says that he merely appears to be good before Banquo. But actually, he wants to destroy him, and after destroying Banquo, he will have to express outward grief on his death. For this reason, he needs their help—

> That I to your assistance do make love,
> Masking the business from the common eye
> For sundry weighty reasons. (3.1.123-25)

The doubleness of Macbeth's character is also suggested by various images of clothing in the play, which are connected with the adoption of a new or false role. By the final scenes, the royal robes have become a burden for him. Angus rightly opines that his title hangs about him like 'a giant's robe upon a dwarfish thief'. Now Macbeth finds that his kingship is slipping away from him. His own men start deserting him. Those who follow him do so from a habit of discipline, not out of love and loyalty for him. The difference between appearance and reality is seen in the behavior of his own men. They appear to be faithful towards him. But in their hearts, they have hatred towards him.

Lady Macbeth again and again professes the use of fair appearance to hide the evil motives of heart. It is she, who instigates Macbeth to commit the most foul deed. In her very first speech, when she reads the letter of her husband she says that Macbeth can get kingship only by adopting foul means—

> What thou wouldst highly,
> That wouldst thou holily; wouldst not play false,
> And yet wouldst wrongly win. (1.5.17-19)

She fears the mild and gentle nature of her husband and decides that she will encourage her husband to get the crown by hooks or by crooks. She can go to any extent to get kingship for her husband. She calls upon the evil powers to inspire her with the thoughts of murder and to take away her womanliness. She wants to suppress her womanliness, maternal instincts and kind impulses by the supreme efforts of sheer will. She fills her heart with anger and cruelty, ignores her sex, suppresses her conscience and prepares herself for the murder of Duncan. She asks the night to become darker and darker so that she could not see the wound inflicted by her on Duncan's body.

Lady Macbeth again and again asks Macbeth to hide what's going on in his heart. She impels him to commit the crime, and advises him to look innocent—

> Your face, my thane, is as a book where men
> May read strange matters. To beguile the time,
> Look like the time; bear welcome in your eye,
> Your hand, your tongue; look like th' innocent flower.
> But be the serpent under't. He that's coming
> Must be provided for; and you shall put
> The night's great business into my dispatch; (1.5.59-65)

She advises him to look like a flower which is hiding a serpent in itself. He should express his happiness at the king's arrival, hiding the real feelings of his heart. He should let the people know by his gestures that he is welcoming Duncan to his castle. She also says—

> Only look up clear.
> To alter favour ever is to fear. (1.5.68-69)

She tells her husband that both of them shall be the loudest in expressing their sorrow at the death of Duncan. This they will do in order to deceive others.

> Who dares receive it other,
> As we shall make our griefs and clamour
> roar upon his death? (1.7.77-79)

The hospitality which she shows to Duncan is deceptive. She appears to be an ideal hostess. She says that everything that she and her husband call theirs actually belongs to Duncan. But the reality is that she has already made up her mind to murder him. After the murder of Duncan she smears the faces of sleeping grooms with his blood so that it will seem that they have committed the deed. She asks her husband to put on his dressing gown to show that they were sleeping in their room—

> Get on your nightgown, lest occasion call us
> And show us to be watchers. (2.2.70-71)

When she is informed about Duncan's murder she appears to know nothing about it. It is difficult to decide whether she really faints or not after hearing the news. In the banquet scene, when Macbeth leaves the feast in order to talk to the murderers about Banquo's murder, Lady Macbeth cunningly handles the situation. She tries to convince the guests by saying that her husband often behaves in an unnatural manner and he will be all right after some time. She gives a little lecture to Macbeth on the importance of formalities observed during social dinners as distinguished from private dinners at home. She tells him to be careful in playing the role of a host. Macbeth is nervous and agitated by the sight of Banquo's ghost in the feast. Macbeth guilty mind sees the victim of his crime, as he once saw the dagger leading to the room of Duncan. To this, Lady Macbeth says that he is upset by something which she does not see at all. She says that it is only an illusion caused by his fear—

> O proper stuff!
> This is the very painting of your fear;
> This is the air-drawn dagger which you said
> Led you to Duncan. (3.4.60-63)

As compared to Macbeth, Lady Macbeth is superb in playing the role of the hypocrite in the first crime and in the banquet where the ghost of Banquo appears. Fear and anxiety are clearly reflected from Macbeth's face because of the murderous thoughts and deeds. It is his wife who manages the whole show admirably.

In spite of all her villainy Lady Macbeth cannot be called a she monster. Her words and deeds make us think that she is monstrous. But we must remember that she is one of those who speak daggers but use none. When she wishes to use the dagger, she finds that she cannot do so. She decides to kill Duncan with her own hands. But she could not do so. Her own words reveal her womanly feelings—

> Had he not resembled
> My father as he slept, I had done it. (2.2.12-13)

Her womanly feeling is also seen when she says—

> I have given suck, and I know
> How tender it is to love the babe that milks me.
> (1.7.54-55)

She invokes the evil spirits to fill her heart with direst cruelty. This shows the need to suppress the revolt of her womanly feelings against the thoughts of murder. She succeeds to repress her womanly feelings only for a short time. When the deed is done she gradually breaks down and recedes into the background. Disillusionment and despair prey upon her more and more. She can no longer tell a connected story. The strain of keeping up appearances is too much for her. Thus, we can say that she seems to be monstrous only in her appearance. As the action develops, it is clear that in reality she is a woman with common feminine weaknesses.

King Duncan is described as a saintly king. He is a gracious man scattering large-heartedness and showering dignities upon his nobles and generals. He imagines that such type of policy will bind his people to him by ties of gratitude. But his tragedy is that his graciousness is mistaken. He thinks that love and liberal attitude are enough to win the respect and loyalty of his people. He expects gratitude from those to whom he himself is grateful but finds that he gets ingratitude and treachery in return. Macbeth describes him as a meek, honest and imperial king. But his virtues become his weaknesses. He remarks that the Thane of Cawdor appeared to be so honest and loyal but he is a traitor in reality. He says that no one can judge a person by his appearance only. One can't say who is honest and who is dishonest because it is not written on the face—

> There's no art,
> To find the mind's construction in the face.
> He was a gentleman on whom I built
> An absolute trust. (1.4.12-15)

In order to emphasize the deceptive nature of appearance, this remark of Duncan is immediately followed by the stage-direction 'Enter Macbeth etc.'. He blindly trusts Macbeth. He confers upon him that very title of Cawdor whose treachery he has come to know only a moment before. The poor king could not realize that the new Thane of Cawdor is as treacherous as the previous one. He again and again appreciates his loyalty and honesty. When he reaches Macbeth's castle he is all praises for its paradisal peace and calm. He does not realize that it is mere appearance, the reality is entirely different. It is not a Paradise but a Hell. He could not think that he will be brutally murdered there. The porter scene echoes the same thought. The porter of Macbeth's castle thinks that he is the porter of Hell-gate. He no longer wants to act the part of Hell's gatekeeper:

> Faith, here's an equivocator, that could swear in both the scales against either scale; who committed treason enough for God's sake, yet could not equivocate to heaven. (2.3.10-13)

This may be the irrelevant rambling of a drunkard but it is true. The drunken Porter, indirectly and unknowingly, judges and condemns his master Macbeth who has murdered the king. By his words we feel that Macbeth too is knocking the gate of Hell for his entry into it for he has committed a horrible sin. Macbeth's castle is indeed a Hell for Duncan. He and his wife are the devils who murder their royal guest. Duncan appreciates Lady Macbeth's hospitality and calls her 'our honour'd hostess'. He expresses his gratitude and thanks for the warm welcome given to him by her. He also sends a special gift for her. He behaves like a lamb licking the hands of its butcher. It is dreadful, but it is also dramatically one of the unforgettable poignant touches by which Shakespeare creates an atmosphere of dramatic irony in the play. How full of affection and trust Duncan is! His unqualified trust is the cause of his tragic end.

Macduff and Malcom, two other important characters of the play, are honest characters. After the murder of Duncan, Malcom thinks that after killing Duncan Macbeth will proceed to kill all who stand as his rivals. He is clever enough to judge Macbeth's treachery. He says:

> Let's not consort with them.
> To show an unfelt sorrow is an office
> Which the false man does easy.
> I'll to England. (2.3.134-37)

His brother Donalbain says:

> Where we are,
> There's daggers in men's smiles; the near in blood,
> The nearer bloody. (2.3.138-40)

Both of them run away from the country. But their act helps in the evil designs of Macbeth. He finds it easy to prove that the grooms were hired by Malcom and Donalbain to murder their father. Their flight is taken as the act of traitors afraid of being detected. So here, the appearance is not true. Though for a short time, Macbeth makes people think that they are the murderers. There is another example in the play when Malcom appears to be wicked and cruel before Macduff. This he does only to judge Macduff's real-self. Malcom is suspicious about Macduff's motives. He imagines that Macduff might be one of the agents of Macbeth, sent to lure him to Scotland where it would be easy to kill him. He pretends to play the role of a vicious person. He assumes a false appearance and tells Macduff that he is not worthy of being the ruler of Scotland because he is many times more vicious than Macbeth. He says that his lust has no limit. Its depth could not be filled with all the women of Scotland. In addition to his lustfulness, he is very covetous and greedy. If he becomes the king, he will destroy the nobles to get their estates and money. He has none of the virtues which are desirable in a king such as kindness, humility, patience, honesty, heroism and endurance. Macduff is very honest and loyal towards his country. To Malcom's statements, he gives a fair response. He says that Malcom can do whatever he wants to do when he becomes the king of Scotland. He may secretly enjoy as much as he likes, and outwardly he may appear as a self-controlled person. He suggests that it is possible in the world to be a lustful person, hiding one's lust beneath a mask of temperance. The reference is to the hypocrisy of so-called great men. When Malcom's mind is free from all suspicions about Macduff, he places himself entirely under Macduff's guidance and takes back whatever evil he has spoken about himself. He contradicts his statements about the vices which are foreign to his nature. Thus, he shows doubleness of character only to judge Macduff's loyalty—

> The taints and blames I laid upon myself
> For strangers to my nature. I am yet
> Unknown to woman, never was forsworn,
> Scarcely have coveted what was mine own,
> At no time broke my faith, would not betray

The devil to his fellow, and delight
No less in truth than life.
My first false speaking
Was this upon myself. What I am truly
Is thine and my poor country's to command:
(4.3.124-33)

The picture of Macduff and his family is set within glorious contrast with that to Macbeth. Macduff's family represents loyalty while Macbeth's family represents treachery and ingratitude. Macduff's patriotism is nobly dramatized. It is his intense love of his country which causes him to sacrifice his wife and children and leave them at the mercy of cruel Macbeth. But he is wrongly judged by the people. Ross tells Lady Macduff that the flight of Macduff has given rise to all sorts of rumours about his treachery. He tells her in veiled language that he is afraid that his flight would endanger the lives of his wife and children. Ross knows that the murderers are just outside the castle and they will soon murder Lady Macduff and her children. But his courage fails when he wishes to tell her plainly about it. So, he talks indirectly telling her that they are in a state of crisis. Lady Macduff also misunderstands her husband. Though she is a devoted and faithful wife, yet Macduff's sudden flight without informing her annoys her. She tells her son that his father is dead for him because he does not love him anymore. He has run away leaving his wife and his children behind. She could not realize that her husband has run away not because of fear but because he loves his country more than his family. Moreover, he could never think that his wife and children would be killed in this way.

The Witches are equivocating fiends whose words appear to have one particular meaning at the time when they are spoken, but later on it is felt that the real meaning of their words is entirely different. They tell Macbeth that he need have no fear till Birnam woods move to Dunsinane and that no man born of woman can harm him. The result is that Macbeth is deceived because he has a wrong sense of security. It's too late that he realizes that these words are deceptive. Birnam woods appear to be moving, but this is not the reality. Actually, they are the branches of trees which Malcom's army uses to deceive Macbeth's army. In this way they could hide themselves. Macbeth's spies could not judge their real numbers. Macduff, who kills Macbeth, can be called as a man not born of a woman because he was taken out of his mother's womb through an operation. Macbeth now realizes the true nature of Witches. In reality, their words have entirely different significance. Their words lead him to hope that no one can defeat him, but the hope is deceptive. They make a fool of him.

2
Hamlet

Hamlet is in many respects Shakespeare's problem play and one of the problems that it presents is that of dating. Many external and internal evidences taken together with stylistic criteria also in mind lead to the conclusion that the play was composed between 1600-1601. Towards the close of the twelfth century, the story of Hamlet is told for the first time in the Latin 'Historia Danica' of Saxo Grammaticus, a Danish historian. The story of Amleth, as told by Saxo, provides the basis for Shakespeare's *Hamlet.* He must have got a few valuable suggestions from Belleforest who rendered Saxo's story in French in the fifth volume of his *Histories Tragiques*, printed in 1570. There is a lost 'Hamlet' ascribed to Thomas Kyd. It was once very popular. Shakespeare might have been asked by his company to turn out a rival 'Hamlet'. He could have been influenced by Kyd's 'Hamlet' as well as by his *Spanish Tragedy*. The sources may be varied and numerous from where Shakespeare borrowed certain events and characters but he made the play entirely his own. It is due to his inventive genius and literary caliber.

Shakespeare, in his plays, deals with various issues. His themes are varied. In *Hamlet* also the issues or the themes he deals with are—'appearance versus reality', 'kingship', 'ingratitude', 'mighty ambition', 'lust for political power', 'many facets of love', 'friendship', 'contrast between good and evil', 'destiny &

fate', 'stoicism and courage', 'madness' and so on. In this play Shakespeare tends to observe life and comment on it.

The most important issue or the theme in the play is the contrast between 'appearance and reality'. The atmosphere of the play is full of confusion, corruption and decay. The play contains a great deal of corruption, sickness and disease imagery. The hero of the play is entangled in a mud of uncertainty, confusion and misunderstanding. The more he struggles hard to come out of it, the more he gets into it. Hamlet, the hero is not certain of how his father died, whether his mother whom he loves so much knows or not of the murder, if the ghost of his father telling the truth, if his friends are faithful towards him and if the love of Ophelia true for him. He cannot decide whether he should be guided by what he sees or he should try to read between the lines. It's a play in which the most questions are asked and the fewest answered. Not only does this play raise many questions but it also presents several riddles. The hero's language is often riddling. When he puns, his puns have receding depths in them. His first speech can be taken up as an example—

> A little more than kin, and less than kind. (1.2.65)

His utterances in madness, even if they are wild, are discovered to be pregnant by Polonius. His madness itself is riddling. His mind plays restlessly about his world turning up one riddle upon another. To him, man himself is the most mysterious creature, the greatest riddle of all. He is aware of the fact that he has a mystery in him and that the spies of the king want to discover that mystery. Again and again we find him questioning himself why he does not take revenge in spite of the fact that there are the most serious provocations to do so. Mystery is present in the countless explanations which are given for Hamlet's delay, his madness, his father's Ghost, his treatment of Polonius, Ophelia, and his mother. Political intrigue, treachery, deception and faithlessness are the important features of this play but even the masters of these traits, Claudius and Polonius, find that events run away with them. They find that their intrigue and deception cannot save them from death. Thus the atmosphere of the play and the main features of it convey the idea that nothing in *Hamlet* is what it seems to be. Everything in the play can be interpreted and explained in many different ways.

Freud identifies the Oedipal relationship as a general event in childhood which can explain the gripping power and enigma of Hamlet. He says that the tragedy of Hamlet has been admired for three hundred years without its meaning being discovered or its author's motives guessed. In his *The Interpretation of Dreams* (1900) he elaborates on the guilt feelings aroused in Hamlet by his incestuous desire for his mother and his wish to displace his father. In *Oedipus Rex* this wish is acted out whereas in *Hamlet* it is repressed. The play gives the audience's repressed desires a way to satisfy themselves imaginatively. Hamlet is haunted by a complex which he is unable to resolve thus inviting self-analysis but the audience, deeply moved, identifies in Hamlet's tragedy their own secret history. Hamlet's own repressed desires are projected in Claudius' murdering of king Hamlet and marrying his wife. When he becomes Hamlet's stepfather, Hamlet is free to direct his own death wish against him without repression. Now he may safely punish his uncle as though punishing himself for his illicit feelings towards his mother and against his father. Freud says with pride that the conflict in Hamlet is so effectively concealed that it was left for him to unearth it. He was forever busy in penetrating secrets. After the Oedipal interpretation of the play, no one goes back to Hamlet the same way. There are subtle changes in our perspective and our reception of the play.

The form of the play *Hamlet* is deceptive. On a superficial view *Hamlet* may be considered a revenge-play. It contains all the basic elements of a revenge play. The ghost of the dead king appears and reveals the identity of the murderer, the task of revenge is entrusted to Hamlet, who accepts it as a sacred duty. He faces many difficulties in the performance of his task. Finally, he is successful in completing his task but in the process both the avenger and the avenged are killed. Plots, counterplots, treachery, assumed and real madness, fighting, bloodshed are found in the play. But if we closely study the play, we find that it is not a typical revenge play in the sense of the term. It deals with a tragic problem of life. The problem is that of a divided mind. It's a play that deals with a conflict between faith and reason, between lofty idealism and sordid realities of life. In Hamlet's case, the solution of this conflict or the problem becomes very difficult because of his character and the particular situations in which he is placed. Shakespeare has given an intellectual and emotional re-orientation to the entire play. Hamlet's thoughts on the problems of life and death, the existence of evil in society, death of friendship, loyalty, sincerity in the world, the influence of destiny or fate on human life—all these enhance the intellectual appeal of the play. Shakespeare has woven into the play complex threads of contrast of character and ideas which elevate it much above the common plays of Revenge genre. The artistic devices, language, the universal issues it deals with, the complex nature of its hero—all these features lift 'Hamlet' much above what is conventionally termed 'Revenge Tragedy'.

Belief in the supernatural and wonder at the inexplicable mysteries of death was largely shared by people during the Elizabethan Age. Shakespeare makes effective use of these popular superstitions and beliefs of his time. In Hamlet, the supernatural appears in the form of the Ghost. The Ghost in Hamlet is a solemn, majestic figure which is at once mysterious and real. The way it haunts at the dead hour of night gives the audience a mysterious thrill of the strange and unknown. But it is not a product of Hamlet's excited imagination. It appears on successive nights and is seen by several people. It is absolutely real and has an objective existence. Horatio, the sceptic does not at first believe in the existence of the Ghost. He attributes it to his friend's fantasy. Marcellus comments on Horatio's scepticism—

> Horatio says 'tis but our fantasy,
> And will not let belief take hold of him,
> Touching this dreaded sight, twice seen of us;
> Therefore I have entreated him along
> With us to watch the minutes of this night,
> That, if again this apparition come.
> He may approve our eyes and speak to it. (1.1.23-29)

To this, Horatio says

> Tush, tush ! 'twill not appear. (1.1.30)

To Horatio, when he at first hears about the Ghost, it appears to be an imaginary thing and the fantasy of his friends. He could not think that it is real. When he himself witnesses its appearance with his own eyes, he cannot disbelieve his eyes. He accepts the fact that it resembles the late King of Denmark in every respect.

The question whether the Ghost in a subjective or an objective entity still remains a problem to the critics. In fact, there can be little doubt of the reality and visibility of the Ghost in the opening scene and later when he speaks to Hamlet. Some critics suggest that Shakespeare's characters Macbeth, Brutus and Hamlet, highly gifted with the imagination, are susceptible to the existence of ghosts. Banquo's ghost at the royal banquet might be a hallucination of Macbeth, for neither the ghost addresses Macbeth nor it is visible to anybody else. The guilty mind of Macbeth only sees the ghost. Similarly Caesar's ghost may be the creation of Brutus' imagination, but Caesar's ghost does speak to Brutus. This view which is justified in the beginning is contradicted when the Ghost makes its second appearance in the bed-chamber of Gertrude. Hamlet sees the Ghost but to Gertrude it is invisible. It appears to her that Hamlet, in his insane state of mind, is talking to the airy nothing. She says—

> This is the very coinage of your brain.
> This bodiless creation ecstasy
> Is very cunning in. (3.4.139-41)

If the Ghost here has an objective reality, it should have been seen and heard by Gertrude also. Some critics say that the first apparition is real and the second is imaginary. The first, to Hamlet, is initiative, the second inhibitive. But I don't agree that in one case the Ghost is real and in another unreal. The fact that the queen does not see the Ghost does not disprove its existence. According to the beliefs of Elizabethan audience, a Ghost could make itself visible to some and invisible to others according to its choice and intention. By keeping the state of Hamlet's mind in view, we cannot think that the Ghost is merely a hallucination. The audience and the readers should not suppose such a thing because the Ghost proves his identity by showing the same traits as were visible on his first appearance—the same stress on the duty of remembering and the same concern for the queen. A.C.

Bradley rightly opines in his *Shakespearean Tragedy*—"The idea of later critics and readers that the Ghost is an hallucination is due partly to failure to follow the indications first noticed, but partly also to two mistakes, the substitution of our present intellectual atmosphere for the Elizabethan, and the notion that, because the queen does not see and hear the Ghost, it is meant to be unreal. But a ghost, in Shakespeare's day, was able for any sufficient reason to confine its manifestation to a single person in a company; and here the sufficient reason, that of sparing the queen is obvious" (Bradley 1961: 111-12).

It may be said that the Ghost, not being seen by the queen, has its moral significance. It suggests that the woman has strayed so far from the path of honour that she is unable to receive spiritual visions. It also indicates the intimate relationship between father and son so that the son alone is admitted to the inner secrets and the absolute breach between husband and wife. The Ghost is invisible to the queen because he wants to spare her the knowledge of the murder. The Ghost, therefore, is real and objective and yet carries a sense of mystery with its majestic personality.

There is a mystery not only in the existence of the Ghost but also in the purpose behind this apparition. The Ghost is a portentous figure whose real motive can be understood, not by all, but only by his own son, the young Hamlet. Horatio, Marcellus, Bernardo have a belief that several supernatural phenomena take place before a calamity and the apparition indicates some great disaster to the state of Denmark. It can be a precursor of war. Horatio says—

> In what particular thought to work I know not;
> But, in the gross and scope of mine opinion,
> This bodes some strange eruption to our state. (1.1.67-69)

They are not convinced of his good nature and prevent Hamlet from following the Ghost. Marcellus stops him by saying—

> Look with what courteous action
> It waves you to a more removed ground.
> But do not go with it. (1.4.60-62)

Horatio also expresses his opinion—

> What if it tempt you toward the flood, my lord.
> Or to the dreadful summit of the cliff
> That beetles o'er his base into the sea,
> And there assume some other horrible form,
> Which might deprive your sovereignty of reason
> And draw you into madness? Think of it;
> The very place puts toys of desperation,
> Without more motive, into every brain
> That looks so many fathoms to the sea
> And hears it roar beneath. (1.4.69-78)

Hamlet does not doubt the Ghost's existence, he doubts only his authenticity. But when he hears the whole story of his father's murder from the Ghost, he calls him 'an honest Ghost'. With the Ghost's description of the nature of Claudius and Gertrude, Hamlet as well as the spectators come to know them in their true colours. Now, the fair appearance they put on could not hide the treachery of their hearts. The Ghost describes to Hamlet, his murder and tells how Claudius, Hamlet's uncle, incestuous, adulterate and a villain seduced his mother with his wit. He says that it has been reported that a serpent bit him while he was sleeping in the garden. So, all the people of Denmark were deceived by a fabricated story of his death. The appearance is made the reality by Claudius. But, actually, the serpent that bit the king was his own brother Claudius. The Ghost also reveals the true nature of the queen. He says that the queen appears to be a virtuous woman. But in reality, she is a faithless woman. She has the semblance of a virtuous woman. The Ghost says that a virtuous person will never be tempted to go after evil even if evil assumes the shape of angels to tempt him. In the same way, an evil person will go after evil, even if virtue were to be his partner in life. There is a perversion of taste and values. Gertrude is like that lustful person who is never satisfied by lawful indulgence in pleasure and is tempted to seek what is foul and evil. It appears from the Ghost's words that he hates her a lot and wants to punish her for her faithlessness. But, actually, his true love for the queen stops him to do so. He is surely annoyed with her but does not want to cause any harm to her. He asks Hamlet not to hurt her in anyway. Thus, the love of King Hamlet for his wife was true. He was wholly devoted to her. Even after his death, his Ghost shows warm sentiments for her.

As contrary to her husband's pure love, Gertrude's love for the king is not pure. She is not a devoted and faithful wife as she appears to be. She weeps bitterly when her husband dies to make a show off of her grief. She may well have wept the more bitterly because she had been false to him. Within two months, she marries her brother-in-law, Claudius, and is still the Queen. There is no hint in her of any remorse for the past. She is very happy with her second husband. Sometimes, she is conceived as one who is dead to all spiritual values. There is nothing like conscience in her. She is spiritually and morally blind until Hamlet holds a mirror before her in which she witnesses the blackness of her soul. Even after that, we cannot say that Hamlet is able to open her eyes to the truth about her second husband's deceitfulness. In spite of Hamlet's references to his uncle as a murderer, she really does not seem to suspect the truth until the very end of the play, for she never shows, in word or in deed that she has drawn any such conclusion from what she has heard from her son.

Some critics say that she entered into adulterous relations with Claudius while her husband was living and that she may have participated in the crime. But I don't agree with this view. She is certainly a weak woman, but not an evil one. In the beginning of the play, it appears that she has knowledge of her husband's murder. But this is not the reality. She is innocent of her husband's murder and it is proved by her reaction to 'The Mouse Trap'. She is angry with Hamlet for upsetting Claudius but does not show any sign of herself having a guilty conscience. She says of the Player-Queen—

> The lady doth protest too much, methinks. (3.2.225)

This means that the Player-Queen asserts faithfulness to her husband so extravagantly that one is compelled to suspect it. Bradley remarks—"The queen was not a bad-hearted woman, not at all the woman to think little of murder" (Bradley 1961: 135).

Actually, Gertrude has a soft animal nature, unimpressive, self-centered and very shallow. She loves to be happy and it pleases her to see others happy. Her over-hasty second marriage shows her to be a sensual, easy going woman, with no depth of character. The Ghost's revelation makes it clear that she is not a devoted wife to her first husband. It's her inconstancy which makes Hamlet generalize—

> Frailty, thy name is woman (1.2.146)

About her weakness, Dowden says—"The timid, self-indulgent, sensuous, sentimental queen is as remote from true woman's virtue as Claudius is from the virtues of royal manhood" (Dowden 1970: 250). The Ghost blames her for her weakness and sensuality but never accuses her of adultery or of participation in the crime. His words imply that after his death, she was easily seduced by Claudius. His words do not establish her relationship with Claudius even when her first husband was alive. Her love for Hamlet is true. She knows the cause of her son's sorrow—his father's death and her over-hasty marriage. But her love is selfish rather than sympathetic. She wishes the cause of Hamlet's madness to be the ecstasy of love. She is not troubled by any shame for her conduct. It is pleasant for her to sit upon the throne and see smiling faces around her. For her, it is foolish and unkind in Hamlet to grieve all the time for his father instead of marrying Ophelia and leading a comfortable life. Her advice to Hamlet is—

> Good Hamlet, cast thy nighted colour off,
> And let thine eye look like a friend on Denmark.
> Do not for ever with thy vailed lids
> Seek for thy noble father in the dust.
> Thou know'st 'tis common—all that lives must die.
> Passing through nature to eternity. (1.2.68-73)

She is innocent of Claudius' wickedness and she realizes his true nature only in the end when she drinks the poisoned wine. It's too late that she discovers the treachery of Claudius' heart hidden behind a fair appearance. When the king tries to pretend that she is merely swooning at the sight of blood, she collects her energies to deny it and to warn Hamlet—

> No, no the drink, the drink!—O my dear Hamlet!
> The drink, the drink! I am poison'd. (5.2.301-02)

Claudius can be ranked with the master villains in the plays of Shakespeare like Edmund and Iago. He is a hypocrite and a scheming rogue who can stoop to any means and ways to achieve his selfish ends. Claudius is a schemer, a flatterer, a murderer and a usurper. He commits three crimes in one stroke. He poisons Hamlet, the king, deprives him of his kingdom, and commits adultery and incestuous marriage with his wife. It is from what the Ghost tells Hamlet that we learn the kind of man Claudius is—

> Ay, that incestuous, that adulterate beast,
> With witchcraft of his wits, with traitorous gifts—
> O wicked wit and gifts, that have the power
> So to reduce ! —won to his shameful lust
> The will of my most seeming virtuous queen. (1.5.41-45)

Sweet on tongue, he has abundance of poison in his heart. He looks like an innocent flower, but he is a serpent under it. Hamlet says of him—

> O villain, villain, smiling, damned villain!
> My tables—meet it is I set it down
> That one may smile, and smile, and be a villain;
> At least I am sure it may be so in Denmark. (1.5.106-09)

Throughout the play, he plays the part of a hypocrite. He speaks and does everything on the grounds of his own safety. He murders the king in such a way that it appears to everyone that the king died a natural death. He murders his brother and yet speaks of him as 'Hamlet, our dear brother!' He makes a show off of his grief over his brother's death in his speech from the throne. He behaves in a dignified manner when he presides at the council. He usurps Hamlet's right to the throne and yet speaks of his affection as that of a father towards his son. He wants to keep Hamlet under his strict watch to observe his deeds and control him. But he begs him to stay with him on the grounds of love and affection. He says flattering words to Hamlet—

> Here, in the cheer and comfort of our eye,
> Our chiefest courtier, cousin, and our son. (1.2.116-17)

The clash between Hamlet and Claudius soon begins, but it does not come into open. Claudius sets Hamlet's friends as spies to watch his actions. When needed he himself becomes a spy to watch him. With the advice of Polonius, he employs Ophelia as a decoy. He sends Hamlet to England to get rid of him but he pretends to have a tender regard for his personal safety. He is so wicked that he sends a message to the King of England to murder Hamlet. Claudius has honey on his tongue but a knife in his hand. He is a hypocrite in words and a good schemer in action. His crafty schemes are seen throughout the play. He very cunningly overcomes the anger of Leartes, and uses him as a means to carry out his plans effectively. Though bewildered by his unexpected revolt, he tackles the situation with his speech on the divinity of royal birth. He says that God will protect the body of a king against all dangers. No human being, however treacherous, can harm a royal person. Is Claudius, a murderer and a usurper to the throne, a rightful representative of Divine power on earth? He suspects the reality of Hamlet's madness and is convinced that his insanity has nothing to do with love. When Hamlet kills Polonius, he suspects that the blow was meant for him. He succeeds in all his actions except when he plans to kill Hamlet in England. After this, his scheming loses its efficacy and his plans turn against him to bring about his death. He dies at a time when he feels himself safe in his court.

Claudius keeps a fair exterior and an extraordinary self-possession. When he is at prayer we have a glimpse into his inner being. It is not all well there. He is not a seasoned villain as he appears to be. He cannot pray to be forgiven for his crime for he is still possessed of those things for which he did the murder—his crown and his queen. He appears to be very strong and self-controlled. It appears that he has no conscience at all. But when we observe him at prayer, we see that his conscience pricks him for the crime he has committed. He realizes—

> O, my offence is rank, it smells to heaven;
> It hath the primal eldest, curse upon't—
> A brother's murder! (3.3.36-38)

At least, he is not a hypocrite to himself. He knows who he is. He is clear-eyed and conscious of his limitations. He is inwardly sure that hell is reserved for him. In his soliloquy he is not the smiling villain that he throughout the play is. When he is tested in the play scene, he tries to keep his nerve all right. But he is not able to hide his dirty conscience and falls into the trap of the play arranged by Hamlet. He tries to hide the disturbance of his heart but he fails to do so. The true reality defeats the false appearance. One good quality in him is that his love for Gertrude is deep and genuine. Though their relationship is condemned by Hamlet as carnal and lascivious yet it is true that Claudius loves her very much. His love is not false as it appears to Hamlet. He reveals his heartly feeling for the Queen to Leartes—

> She is so conjunctive to my life and soul,
> That, as the star moves not but in his sphere,
> I could not but by her. (4.7.14-16)

He could not punish or kill Hamlet openly for it would hurt Gertrude. Thus, we can say that morally he is not as great a monster as he is generally made out to be.

Like other problems, the Hamlet-Ophelia relationship has given rise to a lot of controversy. In this relationship, the reality is not what appears to be. It is very much different. Hamlet makes love to Ophelia in an honourable fashion but he seems to have made a wrong choice. Ophelia could not be a fit companion for him in his life. It seems from the beginning that her love for Hamlet is not true. She has been criticized for reporting to her father Hamlet's strange visit and behaviour, for showing her father one of Hamlet's letters and for telling her father the whole story of their courtship. She is directed in her love affair by her father and does whatever he wants her to do. By the advice of her father, she returns the gifts given to her by Hamlet and refuses to meet him. She even allows herself to be used as a snare by which Hamlet's secrets may be discovered. She offers no protest when her father bids her to play her part of dissimulation, reading a book. Polonius says—

> ...Read on this book;
> That show of such an exercise may colour
> Your loneliness. —We are oft to blame in this:
> 'Tis too much prov'd, that with devotion's visage

> And pious action we do sugar o'er
> The devil himself. (3.1.44-49)

Her love was not such that Hamlet could derive strength from it. It was not such that could enable her to understand him. The queen hopes in vain that her virtues will bring Hamlet back to his normal state of mind. So, from her conduct, it appears that Ophelia is not a faithful lover. She deserts Hamlet when he needs her the most. But this is not the reality. Actually, she has fallen in love with Hamlet and he with her. She devotes herself heart and soul to him without making any effort to conceal her love. There is no cunning, no deceit and no coyness about her. Her brother, Leartes, who himself is frivolous and shallow, appreciates the purity of Ophelia and tells the priest who objects to a Christian burial for her—

> And from her fair and unpolluted flesh
> May violets spring ! I tell thee, churlish priest,
> A ministering angel shall my sister be,
> When thou liest howling. (5.1.233-36)

Her very innocence stands in her way to have a personality of her own. In all things she obeys her father, no matter how much it pains her to go against her own inclinations. She does all innocently, without knowing the consequences of her actions, and with a view of remedying Hamlet. She thinks that her rude behaviour towards Hamlet may be the cause of his gloom and later his madness. She is too innocent to understand Hamlet's grief over his mother's conduct. She observes his mental turbulence without comprehending its cause. Most probably when she tells a lie to Hamlet, she does so because that is what her father, who is listening from his place of concealment, expects her to say. Her love is true but she could not make a show off of her sentiments for Hamlet. She could not express her love in words. The problem with her is that she fails to be a source of strength to Hamlet. Her true love does play some part in her loss of sanity. Unlike the assumed madness of Hamlet, Ophelia's insanity is not a matter of appearance only. It is true.

Much of the misunderstanding about Hamlet's character arises from an imperfect understanding of his affair with Ophelia.

It appears that his love for Ophelia is not true. He does not trust her because he could not tell his real problem to her and take her to his side. If his love had been true, he would have told her everything about his state of mind. He pours abuse upon the unoffending Ophelia and uses dirty language towards her in the play-scene. But this is not true. It's not that having once loved Ophelia, Hamlet ceases to do so. He continues loving her but do not have her know it. The depth of his love is shown by the picture of the agony he suffers at taking leave of her, when—

> He rais'd a sigh so piteous and profound
> As it did seem to shatter all his bulk
> And end his being. (2.1.94-96)

He feigns madness before her perhaps with a view to prepare her for the breaking off of the love intercourse which has no place in the serious business which he has to do. Perhaps his other purpose is to produce an impression of madness which he wants Ophelia to convey to her father and through him to the King. He puts on an antic disposition, yet his distress at this time is real because Ophelia's breaking off with him must have upset him a lot. He loves her sincerely but she disappoints him because of her weaknesses. She is used as a tool by the King and Polonius but Hamlet sees through the whole game. Perhaps, he had overheard Polonius' plot to employ Ophelia as a decoy. Her pretence of reading a devotional book, when in fact she is waiting for him, is enough to rouse his suspicion. He tests her by asking where her father is. When she tells a lie, he becomes sure that she is on the side of his enemy. He insults Ophelia by his obscene remarks because of his hatred of his mother's behaviour and of what he considers as Ophelia's betrayal. Perhaps the cruelest thing he says to her in the nunnery-scene is that he has never loved her but only lusted after her. But this is not true. He challenges Leartes to any kind of competition to prove that he loves Ophelia better. To Leartes' extravagant show of grief on her death he says—

> I love'd Ophelia: forty thousand brothers
> Could not, with all their quantity of love,
> Make up my sum. (5.1.263-65)

There is no point to think that at such a tragic moment, Hamlet would indulge in extravagant meaningless talks. It's a genuine explanation of his former love for Ophelia. The reality is that he is compelled to give up thoughts of love when he is charged with the duty of avenging her father's murder. The thought that she has deserted and betrayed him helps him in the process. After her death, his old love returns to him like a flood when he sees Leartes' extravagant show of brotherly love.

Hamlet's madness is feigned and not real. There is some ground for the view that Hamlet has really gone mad. When he appears for the first time, he is not in a normal state of mind. His father's death and his mother's over-hasty marriage produce in him a disgust for the affairs of life. After the Ghost's revelation, he sinks into a morbid state of mind which is very near insanity. Ophelia's description of his strange appearance and behaviour to her supports this view. Her description gives Polonius the idea that Hamlet has lost his mind on account of his disappointment in love. Hamlet's conversation with Polonius in Act II, Sc. II, also supports the theory that he is really mad. He calls Polonius a fishmonger and insults him with obscene remarks on his daughter, Ophelia. His talk with his friends Rosencrantz and Guildenstern on the honesty of the world, his talk with Ophelia in the nunnery-scene in which he insults her and advises her to join a convent to escape breeding sinners and his obscene talk with her in the play scene—all are taken to prove that he has lost his reason. Ophelia says—

> O! what a noble mind is here o'er thrown! (3.1.150)

Hamlet's act of killing Polonius is another instance given to support that his madness is real. Not knowing the identity of a person who is hiding behind the arras, he takes it to be Claudius, draws his sword and kills the person. Only afterwards does he find out that it is Polonius. Had he been in his real senses, he would not have acted in this heartless manner. His strange behaviour at Ophelia's funeral shows the genuineness of his madness. The queen explains to Leartes Hamlet's outbursts of passion—

This is mere madness;
And thus awhile the fit will work on him;
...His silence will sit drooping. (5.1.278-82)

But all these evidences do not prove his madness to be real. As against this, there are a lot of evidences to show that he is not really mad but pretends to be mad. He acts normally when he chooses to and in the presence of those with whom it is safe to do so. After the Ghost's revelation, he tells to Horatio and Marcellus that he may put on an 'antic disposition' and behave in an eccentric manner—

As I perchance hereafter shall think meet
To put an antic disposition on... (1.5.171-72)

He feels that the pose of a madman will help him to carry out his purpose of avenging his father's death without alarming his enemies. When he is talking to Polonius, Polonius realizes—

Though this be madness, yet there is method in't. (2.2.205-06)

Claudius, the shrewd man, suspects the authenticity of Hamlet's madness. When Polonius describes the disappointment in love as the cause of his madness, Claudius after observing Hamlet says—

Love! His affections do not that way tend;
Nor what he spake, though it lack'd form a little
Was not like madness. (3.1.162-64)

Rosencrantz and Guildenstern suspect that it is a crafty madness. Only Ophelia and his mother believe in his madness. Hamlet enacts the *Mouse Trap* play to confirm Claudius' guilt. He and Horatio observe the king's reaction carefully. Only a man of wisdom could plan everything systematically and arrive at the expected conclusion. In the bed-chamber of Gertrude, when he criticizes his mother for her frailty and wickedness, her conscience is awakened. No madman's words could be so effective. All his speeches when he is alone or when he is with Horatio, whom he has taken into confidence, are the utterances of a man who has exceptionally powerful intellect. All his soliloquies are coherent and logical and have a depth of thought. His soliloquies express ideas which go straight to every thinking man's heart because of their universal appeal. Through them we come to know about the inner Hamlet, his feelings for others and about himself. The words, ideas and feelings expressed by him cannot be those of a mad man, though they do reflect the agony of a sensitive soul. Hamlet's comments on Yorick's skull and on the other skull, which might be that of a politician or a lawyer, are sensible and full of meaning. His behaviour towards Ophelia cannot be regarded as that of a madman. Perhaps his rudeness towards her is a part of his strategy to put on an 'antic disposition'.

Shakespeare never intended to represent Hamlet as insane. There is a lot of eccentricity in him, a lot of fantastic thinking, a lot of imagination, and a lot of wild phrases. But these elements do not constitute madness. It would be better to think that he is not really mad but there is a vein of abnormality in him. He becomes somewhat morbid due to his father's death and his mother's marriage with an unworthy man. This morbidity deepens with the shock of Ghost's revelation, Ophelia's disloyalty, and his own incapacity to take the revenge.

Hamlet actually feigns madness as a measure of self-defense. His madness is a screen under which he can watch the King and wait for an opportunity for revenge. Dowden opines—"He assumes madness as a means of concealing his actual disturbance of mind. His over-excitability may betray him; but if it be a received opinion that his mind is unhinged, such an excess of over-excitement will pass unobserved and unstudied.... To be in the presence of all and yet to be hidden,—to be intelligible to himself and a perplexity to others, to be within reach of everyone, and to be himself inaccessible, that would be an enviable position!" (Dowden 1970: 144-45).

The theme of illusion and reality is also seen in various soliloquies, incidents and situations related to Hamlet. Gertrude consoles him by saying that death is common and asks him—

> If it be,
> Why seems it so particular with thee? (1.2.75-76)

The word 'seems' breaks his silence for he takes it to denote hypocrisy. He says that in his case it is not the appearance of sorrow but the real sorrow. His grief is the grief in the 'real' sense for he does not believe in falsehood and false appearances. He adds that it is not his dark cloak, nor the black customary suit of mourning, nor his heavy sighs, nor the dejected look on his face which shows his grief. These outward signs may be 'seeming' for people like the King and the Queen. People may think that they are artificial. But his sorrow is internal which cannot be shown outside. All the outward signs of grief are insignificant as compared to his inner grief, which he can reveal to nobody. In these lines, the character of Hamlet is made quite clear. His aversion to artificial and hypocritical behaviour is shown here. The word 'seem' is thematically relevant. Hamlet agrees to stay in Denmark where Claudius is king and this means he 'seems' to forgive his mother's hasty marriage. He keeps silence but it is very painful to him. He does not express the real feelings of his heart at this moment. When the king and the queen ask him to stay with them, he says that he will obey them as best as he can.

Rosencrantz and Guildenstern appear to be faithful in their friendship with Hamlet but actually they are guided in their actions by Claudius, the King. They speak words of friendship to Hamlet in order to find out what lies in his heart. Very soon Hamlet understands that they are being used as spies to judge his behaviour. He questions them about their visit and makes them admit their real motive. When they tell a lie, he says that their looks betray them and they have not yet learnt the art to dissemble. He says that the whole world seems dishonest to him. The fair framework of the earth seems to him a barren land. The air, the beautiful sky all appear to be evil and poisonous. Denmark seems to him like a prison with many confines, wards and dungeons. It may not be a prison for them. What is good for one can be bad for another. Everything depends upon the people.

In reality, Hamlet is in no doubt of what is evil and what is good. Evil can appear as good for a while. Hamlet, actually, is disgusted with life because of the showy, vicious and wicked people. Besides his mother and uncle, his friends too have deceived him. He is an excellent judge who reads others' minds. Hamlet and his friends talk about ambition—

Guil. : Which dreams indeed are ambition; for very substance of the ambitious is merely the shadow of a dream.

Ham. : A dream itself is but a shadow.

Ros. : Truly, and I hold ambitions of so airy and light a quality that it is but a shadow's shadow. (2.2.256-61)

Hamlet's trouble is that he is disturbed by dreams, that is, the vision of the Ghost which has given him the task of revenge. But his friends misunderstand him and say that his dreams are his ambitions which are useless and unsubstantial. They think that Hamlet is perhaps ambitious, that is, he wants to be the king. When Hamlet is informed about the players' arrival, he shakes hands with Rosencrantz and Guildenstern and bids them welcome to Elsinore. He does not want them feel that he treats the players better than his friends. He adds that he will be courteous in the prescribed way of society and show his welcome as well as feel it. He speaks formal words of welcome to them in spite of judging their true nature.

Hamlet directs the players how to speak and act. He directs them not to move their hands up and down, but requires their gestures to be mild and gentle. Even when they are swept by passion they should acquire and develop a moderation that may make the passion seem natural and harmonious. He instructs them to act modestly to bring out the passion sincerely and not to overdo it. They should be in their good sense to suit the action to the speech and speech to the action. They should not go beyond the limits of nature, for anything overacted becomes contrary to the purpose of acting. The object of the play is to reflect nature, to show virtue in its true colour to represent everything as it really is.

Hamlet plans to stage *The Mouse Trap* play with a definite purpose which is known only to him and his friend Horatio. He makes others think that the play is meant only for the entertainment. The King and the queen are happy to see that he is taking interest in worldly things. But actually, the play is meant to put both Claudius and the Ghost on trial, the former for fratricide and the later for its honesty. He prepares the players, Horatio and himself to catch the conscience of the king. He chooses to sit at Ophelia's feet rather than next to queen, partly to give the idea that his madness is caused by disappointed love but mainly because he could not watch the King's face if he sits next to the queen. The dumb show closely represents the crime of Claudius. But Claudius does not betray his feelings. He pretends as if he has not noticed the remarks about second marriages, which are very offensive. In the actual play also, the King tries hard not to show by his face what he is feeling. But finally, he gets up in the midst of the play when he is unable to hide his guilty conscience. Hamlet discovers the truth. He confirms the Ghost's story, but at the expense of revealing his own knowledge to the King. His behaviour during the play and the lack of taste in choosing a play with such a theme allows the King to cover up his guilt with a show of anger. But Hamlet is very happy to see that Claudius, the thick skinned man who seems to be wholly insensitive to attacks on his senses, is now showing good signs of a bad temper. It happens that his armour of hypocrisy has been hit and pierced and his guilty soul within that armour is hard pressed under a weight of remorse and repentance.

In the nunnery-scene, when Hamlet is suspicious of Ophelia being used as a decoy, he charges her with dishonesty and advises her to guard her beauty with honesty. He says that formerly beautiful women were virtuous but now beauty has degraded the virtuous women. Beauty has the power to transform honesty to vice, but honesty is not forceful enough to make beauty virtuous. He says that a beautiful person never acts honestly. Beauty is so full of temptation that even the most honest person is infected by its deceits. He means that Ophelia is fair only in outward form. She is not honest inwardly. She is allowing her beauty to be used as a tool in the hands of her father and the King. Hamlet also thinks that his mother's beauty may be the means of tempting Claudius to kill his brother and marry her. So, his firm view whether right or wrong, is that women are always vicious and corrupt. He generalizes upon women's tendency to paint their faces in order to hide the inner ugliness of their hearts. He says that women use cosmetics on their faces, talk and walk in affected style and pretend to be innocent to hide their lustful and vicious nature. He advises Ophelia not to get married because even if she is as chaste as ice, as innocent as snow, she will not escape a bad name. She will surely be condemned. Hamlet actually knows that Ophelia is not a wanton girl. But he feels that her innocence is being misused by her father.

When Claudius kneels down to pray, Hamlet seeing him at prayers, hesitates to act, bound by his morality. Ironically, he misses an opportunity to kill his enemy, because Claudius is not able to pray. Hamlet has been deceived by the appearance of a kneeling man. According to Christian theory there is redemption for every repentant soul. But Claudius is not able to repent for his sin. The appearance of repentance is not a reflection of his true state of mind. He only wants to be forgiven. Actually, he is concerned only about his own safety. So, he is not able to pray. Once again appearance is deceptive.

When Hamlet goes to his mother's bed-chamber, he decides that he will use harsh words which are like daggers to her conscience but will not use a real dagger to kill her. He only wants to awaken her conscience. So, his tongue and soul will act contrary to each other. He would rebuke her with words, but will not act upon them—

> I will speak daggers to her, but use none.
> My tongue and soul in this be hypocrites— (3.2.386-87)

He tells his mother that he is cruel only to be kind. By being angry, he seems to be cruel but in fact he is kind to her. He is doing this because he wants her to repent and make herself better. He also says that she should put on the appearance of virtue if she has none of it.

While Hamlet is talking to his mother, Polonius hides himself behind the arras to overhear their conversation. Hamlet stabs him to death thinking him to be Claudius. He thinks that Claudius must be hidden there. Hamlet's speeches about the reality of life and death also reflect the theme of illusion and reality. When Claudius enquires him about the dead body of Polonius, he says that there is no difference between a king and a beggar because both have the same end. Even if birth differentiates one from the other, their end is the same. The ultimate reality is death whatever the appearances may be. The same thought is echoed in the grave-diggers scene when he is musing over the fate of man. He feels sad over man's useless efforts to bring about the growth of his body at great cost only to be eaten up by worms and played with by grave diggers. He asks a skull, whom he calls a jester's skull to go to his lady's chamber and reveal to her the truth that however much she may paint her face, after death she must have a face like this (the jester's skull).

The character of Polonius is also important. No doubt, he is loyal towards Claudius. But his speeches full of flattering words to Claudius, to the Queen and to Hamlet shows his hypocritical nature. He advises his son Leartes on how to prosper in life before his departure for France. He advises him to dress in the best clothes his means allow, for the dress of a man often indicates his character. His advice throws light upon the French people's behaviour of Shakespeare's time. They give more importance to dress unknowing of the truth that appearances are deceptive. On a comic level, Shakespeare depicts the same idea.

Polonius is expert in the art of dissimulation, spying, diplomacy and statecraft. He boasts off his policy of double dealing when he employs Reynaldo as a spy to detect the follies and errors of Leartes in Paris. He tells Reynaldo that if truth is a fish, it can be caught only by the bait of falsehood. If one wants to find out the truth about a person, one must adopt indirect and false ways. One must spy, eavesdrop and pretend to be what one is not. For example—Leartes' truth is to be found out by forging false charges against him. He advises his daughter, Ophelia that she should not believe in Hamlet's vows of love. Hamlet's vows are like the false promises of brokers or agents who put on an outward show of honesty and deceive the customers who are attracted by their professions of honesty. He tells her that in her innocence, she has taken Hamlet's current offerings of love as true offerings, whereas they are not so. He advises her—

> Do not believe his vows; for they are brokers,
> Not of that dye which their investments show,
> But mere implorators of unholy suits,

> Breathing like sanctified and pious bonds.
> The better to beguile. (1.3.127-31)

Leartes' own sister, Ophelia compares him to those hypocritical priests who preach good sermons in the church, ask people to follow the path of virtue, but themselves go on living a licentious and luxurious life. She detects the insincerity and hypocrisy in her brother's long sermon to her about love, chastity, maidenhood, honour and purity of conduct. She knows that he preaches one thing and practices in the opposite manner. She wishes that Leartes too should act upon his words—

> Do not, as some ungracious pastors do,
> Show me the steep and thorny way to heaven,
> Whiles, like a puff'd and reckless libertine,
> Himself the primrose path of dalliance treads
> And recks not his own rede. (1.3.47-51)

One of the minor characters of the play Osric, is the representative of the showy and fashionable courtier of Elizabeth's reign. His desire to distinguish himself from ordinary people leads him to ape, to the best of his ability, the latest fashion set at the court by a few brilliant scholars. In his act of copying, he goes further than his models whose purpose he misunderstands. He mistakes extravagance for wit, ridiculous formality for politeness and affectation for originality. He is superficial and shallow. He fails to see, or pretends not to see, that he is a target for the contempt of Hamlet and Horatio. Hamlet describes him as a man who follows all the fashions and modes of courtly behaviour, bows to everyone, and is most concerned with the ceremonies of fashionable life. Of the true spirit of courtesy, he knows nothing. Inwardly he is empty, outwardly perfect. He does not have the true innate politeness of a real gentleman. He simply puts on the appearance of a gentleman. This description reflects Osric's hypocritical character.

Hamlet's anxiety in the last scene of the play is also in accordance with the theme of appearance and reality. Hamlet fears that he might be misunderstood and misjudged by the people after his death, since no one except Horatio knows the real problem of Hamlet and how he met and solved it. His actions may be interpreted as those of a man who was vain and ambitious, who invented a story of the Ghost in order to kill his uncle to achieve kingship. Horatio alone knows the real Hamlet whose life is a continuous stream of bitterness and disillusion. That is why the dying Hamlet requests Horatio to remain alive in order to tell people his story in all its truthfulness.

3
King Lear

King Lear is one of those four of Shakespeare's tragic plays which are regarded as his greatest works, the other three being *Hamlet*, *Othello* and *Macbeth*. On the basis of all the external and internal evidences taken together with the style, verse-craft and tone of the play, it may be deduced that the play *King Lear* was written towards the end of 1605 or in early 1606.

King Lear is pre-eminently a 'study of evil'. Nowhere has he plumbed more fully the depths of evil than in this play. There are a number of villains and evil doers in the play who are by nature spiteful and malignant. These evil doers are devoid of conscience. They all die without any regret and remorse, with the possible exception of Edmund who, at the last moment, gives way to a sudden impulse of goodness. 'Ingratitude' is also one of the themes of the play. The wicked actions of these villains are a result of the ingratitude of children towards their fathers. Thus, one of the outstanding themes of the play is the 'parent-child relationship'. Lear and Gloucester suffer pains due to the ingratitude of their evil children and are consoled and comforted by the good children. 'Kingship' is also the theme of the play. Lear wants to enjoy the pomp and splendour of kingship without holding any responsibility or duty attached to it. Violation of the duties of kingship is the initial deed from which the tragedy arises. The need to acquire self-knowledge marches alongside the lessons of kingship. The theme of 'justice' also figures out in the play. The question that arises in the play is whether or not Lear in the main plot and Gloucester in the sub-plot receive justice, and whether or not the ending is just. 'Madness' too may be regarded as a theme in the play. In this play we observe the actual madness of Lear, the feigned madness of Edgar, the professional madness of the Fool, and the madness of the elements whose fury aggravates the tragic intensity of the play. The Lear who dies at the end of the play is a different man from the man whom we meet in the opening scene. Lear, at the beginning is a vain, selfish, egoistical, haughty and dictatorial king. Towards the end he becomes gentle, sympathetic and humble. In view of this development in his character, we can regard the theme of the play as the 'redemption of Lear'. Both Lear and Gloucester are purged of their spiritual blindness, stripped of their pomp and superfluity and forced into seeing their real nature, the real nature of others, and the real nature of life. Their misguided actions allow evil to enter the world, which brings punishment for them and introduces death and destruction into the rest of society, affecting guilty and innocent alike.

Critics say that *King Lear* is a 'one word play' and there is a pun with this word. The word which governs the play is 'nature'. The word and its cognates together form the play's theme and unify its plot, characterization, setting, imagery and diction. In the light of its thematic unity many problems regarding the play (the unactable scenes, the vague atmosphere and the unhappy ending) can be better analysed. There is a frequent occurrence of 'nature'. G.B. Harrison observes that apart from the use of animal images, Shakespeare "effected a grim irony by the use of two words which sound throughout the play like the tolling of knell: 'nature' and 'nothing'" (Harrison 1968: 1139). Northrop Frye has made his interpretive observations about "the intricate series of puns on 'nature' in *King Lear* (Frye 1967: 269-70). He emphasizes the connection of "the lower physical nature of the elements" with an "amoral world" to which Edmund adheres in contrast to the "still unspoiled and innocent" world of fools (Lear, Kent, Gloucester and the fools).

Harrison's and Frye's interpretations are correct. By thorough investigation of the contexts in which they occur, we can understand the thematic pattern woven out of the word and its cognates. The word and its cognates (natural, unnatural, unnaturalness, disnatured) appear fifty-one times throughout the play. The meanings are quite ambiguous and different interpretations have resulted. It can refer to either 'Great Nature' or our 'human nature', either physical/material nature or spiritual/mental nature, and either natural affection between parent and child or that between a prince and a subject. Alexander Leggatt points out that we can recognize from them "the doubleness of nature in its dealings with the man: destructive and terrifying on the one hand, beneficent on the other" (Leggatt 1988: 23). The "nature" Leggatt refers to there is of course the Great Nature. This doubleness of nature, though not simply imagined by the characters also reflects the 'doubleness of humanity'. Humanity here means 'human nature'. In *Lear* the good and evil aspects of the Great Nature reflect two similar aspects of human nature. The play is a two-level speech act. It is the playwright's speech act by which the playwright tells us that both the great nature and human nature can be either good or bad at times. When the play is the character's speech act it comprises all the speech acts performed by the characters when they speak. On this level, not a single character seems to realize clearly the correspondence between the 'great nature and human nature'. Lear cries out in wilderness, strips of his clothes to come close to 'nature' himself. Even at his last breath he still cannot understand the similarity between the external nature and our inward nature. He still asks on knowing Cordelia's death: "Why should a dog, a horse, a rat, have life,/ and thou no breath at all?" (5.3.305-06). There is a suggestion that the death of Cordelia at the end is inevitable because as a patriot or as a prudent politician Shakespeare simply cannot let France conquer England. We can also have a 'postcolonial' reading of the text to explain some issues. However, this suggestion ignores the playwright's 'comprehensive soul'.

Lear has two daughters who are 'unnatural' for not having 'a child-like office' (2.1.105). The filial Cordelia has two suitors' of whom one does not, while the other does, have 'natural love for her'. Albany and Cornwall are again opposite to each other by nature; one good and the other evil. The same pattern is found in the family of Gloucester. His 'natural' (bastard) son is actually 'unnatural' (with no filial love) whereas his legitimate son is 'natural' in the sense of showing 'a child like office'. The suggestion that like the great nature, man's nature can be good or bad, is naturally shown by the balancing cast of good and evil characters side by side.

The terms 'natural' and 'unnatural' also denote 'normal' and 'abnormal' when we consider the happenings of the play. We can quote the speech of the king of France—"Sure, her offence/ Must be of such unnatural degree/ That monsters it..." (1.1.217-19).

One of the important themes of the play that I would like to discuss in detail is the 'theme of appearance and reality'. In both the sub-plot and the main plot, the characters are required to distinguish between effusive love which is false and flattering, and genuine love which is deep, pure and silent. Both Lear and Gloucester make a wrong choice. Lear asks for and obtains the illusion of love because he does not know what real love is. Cordelia does know what real love is, and offers him this love. But Lear rejects both her love and her. Goneril and Regan, Lear's two other daughters, know what their father wants and give him that—the illusion of filial devotion. Lear is seen happy with the false love of Goneril and Regan. It's too late when he realizes that he has made a wrong choice, because of which he undergoes a lot of sufferings. In the sub-plot also illusion is made to appear as the reality. Gloucester accepts the illusion instead of the reality when he wrongly judges both Edgar and Edmund.

King Lear is the pivot round which all the actions of the play revolve. He has three daughters Goneril, Regan and Cordelia. Goneril and Regan are married respectively to the Dukes of Albany and Cornwall. Cordelia the youngest is wooed by the Duke of Burgundy and the King of France. Her suitors are staying at the court of Lear to seek her hand. Lear is old and decides to get relief from the business of the state and retire to lead a comfortable and contented life. So he divides his kingdom into three parts to be given to his daughters according to the love they have for their father. He asks his daughters to describe in his court the love they have in their hearts for him. Goneril and Regan describe their deep love for their father in the most eloquent terms. But Cordelia has very little to say. The two elder sisters are amply rewarded for the love they profess. Cordelia comes in for sharp rebuke and banishment from the king's affection and material possessions, property, authority and kingdom.

Freud tries to explain two Shakespearean plays on a single motif as the poet's meditation on the 'role of women' in a man's life and death. By drawing a comparison between *Merchant of Venice* and *King Lear* he interprets the significance of number three. Three pretenders have to choose between three metal caskets. The aged king Lear intends to divide his kingdom among his three daughters. In both the plays the humblest of the three is shown to be the most precious; the plain lead on one side and the plain speechless love of the youngest daughter on the other. He says that gold and silver are loud but lead is dull and so dumb like Cordelia. He understands the uniqueness of the third as her 'dumbness'. Dumbness in psychic life is seen as 'death'. Thus the third woman among whom the choice is made is a 'dead woman'—Death itself or Goddess of Death. No man chooses death in reality and it is 'only by fatality' that a man falls a victim to it. By a wishful reversal, fatality is transformed into free choice. As per mythological tradition, the three daughters in the play resemble the three daughters of Fate. They represent the Law of Nature, the passing of time and the inevitability of death. The scene of *Lear* carrying dead Cordelia in his arms is understood in reverse. In reality she seems to be the Death Goddess who carries away the dead hero from the battlefield of life. She guides the old man renounce love, choose death (third daughter) and make friends with the inevitability of dying. Freud concludes by saying that the play depicts three inevitable relations that a man has with a woman—the mother herself, the beloved whom he chooses in her image and the Mother Earth who finally absorbs him once again.

Feminist criticism questions how women are portrayed, why they are portrayed as such and what effect it has on reader and society as a whole. Gender is a biological construct. Since it is constructed it can be deconstructed as well. Stereotypes are made up ideas that society has about a particular group and they can be destroyed. Shakespeare portrays women as the 'stronger sex' in *King Lear*. In Act 1, Sc. 4 Goneril instructs her father to reduce the number of knights that follow him. Her husband is not in the house and she is the head of the house. When Albany comes, he clearly proclaims that he is innocent and ignorant of everything and he does not keep track of what his wife is doing. When Lear tells her, "thou hast power to shake my manhood thus" (1.4.296) he means that Goneril has enough power over him to make him upset and shattered. The men in this scene are belittled by a woman. Goneril even tells her husband to stay out of it. The demonstration of power by the so-called 'weaker sex' is just a beginning. She uses this power to achieve more sinister goals. Lear's other daughter Regan captures Gloucester and threatens to pluck his eyes for being a traitor. When one of her servants starts fighting Cornwall in order to protect Gloucester, she does not believe her husband can handle the fight. She takes a sword, runs up to the servant and pierces him in the back, thus killing him. She demonstrates her monstrous and evil nature by plucking poor Gloucester's eyes and killing her own servant for no fault of his. The attributes she shows are typically ascribed to males. Shakespeare's audience knows that women can be as violent and power hungry as men. In Act 4, Sc. 2 Goneril tells Edmund that her husband is a coward and she plans him to play the household from now on. She wants Edmund to know how she feels about her husband, so that he will become her lover. Later she poisons Regan, her own sister to get control of the entire kingdom. Shakespeare wants to show his audience that women can achieve whatever men can. He also shows that the power that these women sought destroyed them finally. Perhaps there is a message if these women had acted as women traditionally do, instead of displaying 'manly' attributes, things would have turned out better for them.

The opening scene of the play helps us a lot to study the character of King Lear. The basic defects of his character are revealed to us in this very scene. His weaknesses not only affect himself but so many other persons in the play. He is intolerant, impulsive, short-tempered, autocratic, self-willed and capricious. He lacks foresight and natural wisdom. One of Lear's shortcomings, which I would like to discuss is his love of 'demonstrative scenes'. Lear has already decided upon the division of his kingdom among his three daughters. He has marked the territories to be allotted to them on the map, and he does not propose to make any alteration in this division. Yet he asks his daughters to express their love for him so that he may make the allotment on the basis of what they have to say. Lear's greatest blunder is the result of reasoning from faulty assumptions. He thinks that love can be expressed in words and the verbal expression is necessarily true. It does not occur to him that love can be dissimulated and that the very depth of the love may make one speechless. What he actually wants is the appearance or the show off of love from his daughters. He could not realize that true and genuine love does not need to be demonstrated. It's a thing to be felt and not demonstrated.

Lear also harbours a wrong notion or misconception that as a king and a father he is entitled to all the love of his daughters. If Cordelia says that she loves him only according to her duty, he jumps to the wrong conclusion that she is an unnatural child. He does not want to accept the reality that Cordelia loves him as much as a daughter loves her father. He wants her to demonstrate that illusory love which is not actually present in her heart. What he wants is the illusion of love and not real love. In fact, he knows how much each of his three daughters loves him. He is fully aware of the fact that Cordelia loves him the best and he himself has the greatest affection for her. Inspite of knowing the reality, he does not want to accept it without hearing loud protestations of his daughters' love for him.

It is very much clear from his character that Lear loves flattery. The extravagant statements, expressing their love, made by Goneril and Regan impress him greatly. He is very happy with both of them. Goneril and Regan are shrewd enough to realize what their father wants. On being asked by her father how much she loves him, Goneril gives an eloquent and glowing reply. She says—

Sir, I love you more than word can wield the matter;
Dearer than eye-sight, space, and liberty;
Beyond what can be valued, rich or rare;
No less than life, with grace, health, beauty, honour:
As much as child e'er lov'd, or father found;
A love that makes breath poor and speech unable;
Beyond all manner of so much I love you. (1.1.54-60)

Like Goneril, Regan also expresses her love for her father in glowing terms. She tells her father that the extent of her love for him is the same as that of her sister Goneril but that Goneril in her expression of her love has fallen short and has not been able to express that love. She says that all the other delights which are within the power of the most delicately sensitive part of her nature to enjoy are hateful to her as compared with the delight that she feels in her love for her father. She says—

I am made of that self metal as my sister,
And prize me at her worth. In my true heart
I find she names my very deed of love;
Only she comes too short, that I profess
Myself an enemy to all other joys
Which the most precious square of sense possesses,
And find I am alone felicitate
In your dear Highness' love. (1.1.68-75)

To both Goneril and Regan, Lear allots the territories which he has already reserved for them. He fails to judge the treachery and wickedness of his two daughters' hearts. Goneril and Regan, with their insincere and extravagant expression of love are well enough, but the King waits for something more from his favourite Cordelia—

Now, our joy.
Although our last and least; to whose young love
The vines of France and milk of Burgundy
Strive to be interess'd; what can you say to draw
A third more opulent than your sisters?
Speak (1.1.81-86)

When Cordelia could not demonstrate her love in highflown words, Lear loses his temper. Without giving any further thought to the matter, he disowns her and declares that the share of the kingdom meant for her will be divided equally between Goneril and Regan. It seems proper to him to disinherit and disown her for this imaginary crime. One is surprised at his lack of judgment in believing in the public protestations of love of his two elder daughters, and in not realizing the depth and sincerity of love of his youngest daughter. He fails to realize the worth of Cordelia and the hypocrisy of Goneril and Regan. The poor fellow could not judge Cordelia from her conduct and is misled by her plain truth and lack of hypocrisy and flattery.

Lear lacks the capacity to discriminate between falsehood and honesty, between flattery and plainness, between truth and hypocrisy and between virtue and vice. He mistakes virtue for vice and vice for virtue, truth for falsehood and falsehood for truth, illusion for reality and reality for illusion. He, blinded by his anger against Cordelia, puts himself in the hands and power of his two tiger daughters who are hypocritical, wicked, treacherous, immoral and ungrateful. He even fails to judge his courtier Kent. He refuses to hear the voice of reason and sanity from the noble Earl of Kent when he tries to let his master realize the blunder he is committing. Kent's intervention on Cordelia's behalf infuriates him. He passes an order of banishment against Kent. His treatment of Kent in the opening scene shows the same defect of his character—failure to understand human character. He mistakes Kent's bluntness and straightforwardness for his disobedience and disloyalty. He banishes Kent for offering him truth.

Lear could not judge that Oswald and other servants of Goneril are rude towards him under their mistress's instructions that they are deliberately misbehaving with him. He says—

> I have perceived a most faint neglect of late, which I have rather blamed as mine own jealous curiosity than as a very pretence and purpose of unkindness. (1.4.66-68)

When Goneril speaks harsh words to Lear, he feels that a very small fault in Cordelia seemed so hideous to him. He regrets—

> O most small fault,
> How ugly didst thou in Cordelia show I (1.4.266-67)

Deeply annoyed with Goneril, Lear turns his thoughts towards Regan. He misjudges Regan also. To Goneril, he says that he has another daughter who is affectionate and ready to give him comfort—

> I have another daughter,
> Who, I am sure, is kind and comfortable.
> When she shall hear this of thee, with her nails
> She'll flay thy wolfish visage. (1.4.305-08)

Lear has not the least idea of the disillusionment which is in store for him at his other daughter's house. The Fool tries to make him conscious of the possibility of Regan treating him no better than Goneril has done. But Lear does not seem to agree with Fool's estimate of Regan's character. When he hears that Regan and her husband have refused to meet him, he could not at first believe his ears, but soon he judges their real motive behind a fair excuse—

> Deny to speak with me ! They are sick ! They are weary !
> They have travell'd all the night ! Mere fetches;
> The images of revolt and flying off. (2.4.86-88)

When he finds Kent in the stocks, his doubt gets confirmed—

> This act persuades me
> That this remotion of the Duke and her
> Is practice only. (2.4.111-13)

The device of dramatic irony in drama produces two points of contrasted views. It consists in the use of words by a speaker conveying to the audience, in addition to their own ostensible meaning, another and an ominous one hidden from himself. The secondary meaning may be concealed from the speaker as well as from the person spoken to. In this way whatever appears to be, is not always true. For instance, Lear's professed intention in abdicating royal authority is twofold. He seeks to enjoy peace in his old age and avoid bloodshed among his daughters for the wealth after his death. But actually, just the reverse of this happens. His action brings him a lot of suffering, pain and humiliation and becomes the cause of all the bloodshed and wickedness in the play. It appears to Lear that Regan is in every respect different from her sister Goneril. She will treat him in a nice way as opposed to Goneril. Her eyes offer comfort unlike Goneril's eyes which have a burning effect. She will not close her doors for him. He appreciates her greatly—

> ...thou better know'st
> The offices of nature, bond of childhood,
> Effects of courtesy, dues of gratitude; (2.4.176-78)

But when Lear truly understands her character he speaks just contrary to what he says earlier—

> Those wicked creatures yet do look well favour'd
> When others are more wicked;
> not being the worst stands in some rank of praise.
> (2.4.255-57)

Lear's psychological state can be explained by using Freudian and Lacanian theory. Freud believes that literature is a reflection of the author's unconscious thought. His components of id, ego and superego can be used to analyse Lear's spiral downfall into madness.

Lear's many utterances and hallucinations in his insane state of mind reflect the theme of appearance versus reality. He suffers a lot as a victim of his daughters' ingratitude and of the cruelty of the storm. Facing the cruel stormy night, he declaims against various kinds of crimes that are committed by human beings. He says that the perjurer and the pretender of virtue, who is in reality guilty of forbidden sexual relationships, will tremble with fear in such a night. The base wretch will also tremble in such a night because he has plotted against somebody's life behind a surface appearance which is effective in concealing the truth. Here, we find a reference to the evil-doers who do wicked deeds behind a fair appearance (Act III, Sc. II). In Act III, Sc. IV, Lear's utterances again reflect the same idea when he says that the Bedlam Beggar is the real human being just as he was born. He represents the true state of man because he wears no clothes to change his appearance while all the other people are adulterated because of the clothes they wear. These clothes give them artificial appearance.

In one of Lear's hallucinations he mistakes Gloucester for Goneril. Having seen Gloucester, Lear exclaims that he is face to face with Goneril who has come to him with a white beard on her chin. The white beard of Gloucester makes him think that Goneril has come to him in the disguise of an old man. He recalls the flattering words which his people used to speak to him in order to please him. He now realizes that he was a fool to believe the flattering words of his daughters and others whose only intention was to gain benefits from him by means of flattery. In his very next speech he refers to the most virtuous looking maiden who is essentially lustful and desirous of enjoying sexual pleasure without any restraint. He says that we may think that the woman must be pure and chaste because she is smiling in a silly manner and because her face seems to indicate that she is cold and devoid of any sexual passion. But the fact is that she only pretends to be a shy and virtuous woman. She will shake her head in disapproval at the mention of sexual pleasure. But in reality, this woman may have extreme insatiable sexual hunger. He offers an ironical defense of adultery, copulation and uncontrollable sexual pleasures.

In another speech, Lear says that even the judges who give punishment to thieves in their courts are themselves corrupt because they would change their verdict if they are offered bribes. The very agents of justice may themselves spread injustice in the society. Lear disapproves of the act of the police constable who whips a prostitute for her immorality because the constable himself is inwardly burning with a desire to sleep with her. How can he teach her a moral lesson if he himself is by no means a model of moral uprightness? Lear generalizes that minor vices are clearly seen only in poor people who wear old and ragged clothes. The vices of rich people are hidden behind the robes which they wear. A criminal who is wealthy remains unpunished, while a criminal who is poor cannot escape punishment. He means to say that the weapon of justice discriminates a rich criminal from a poor criminal before hurting him. It hurts the body of the criminal after judging him from his appearance despite the inward wickedness of his heart.

Lear again mistakes appearance for reality when Cordelia's men appear in order to take him away to her. He thinks that these are the men sent by his enemies to catch him. He says—

> No rescue ? What, a prisoner? I am even
> The natural fool of fortune. Use me well;
> You shall have ransom. (4.6.191-93)

After being administered by the doctor in Cordelia's castle, Lear takes enough rest as a result of which his sanity returns to him. When he opens his eyes, he thinks that he has been taken out of his grave. He calls Cordelia, a happy soul dwelling in Heaven. He could not believe that he is alive. He tests the life in him by feeling a pin-prick in his hand. Then he recognizes Cordelia but could not believe that it is she and therefore, feels somewhat doubtful. Lear again mistakes appearance for reality when, in the end, he believes dead Cordelia to be alive. After she has been murdered, Lear, quite pathetically, tries to discern symptoms of life in the body of Cordelia. He seems to think that she is breathing again. He says—

> This feather stirs; she lives. If it be so,
> It is a chance which does redeem all sorrows
> That ever I have felt. (5.3.265-67)

He turns to all those present and asks them to look at Cordelia's lips and face. It seems to him that her lips are moving and that she must, therefore, be yet alive. He dies thinking that Cordelia is coming back to life. Lear has been content to accept illusion as reality though this has only brought him suffering. Now it brings him a moment illusory but final happiness. Illusion has triumphed over reality.

In the two sisters Goneril and Regan, Shakespeare has personified depravity in all its worst forms. Murder, adultery, deceit, treachery—all come to them as naturally as breathing. They have something within them that turns the milk of humanity to venom. What is worse still is that the two monsters are amorous. Their love is even more terrible than their hate. They display extraordinary felicity of tongue in eloquently professing their love hypocritically. Their professions of love and devotion for their father would put to shame the most expert flatterer and self-seeker. Their deceitful words make Lear believe in the love professed by them though at this very moment Kent and Cordelia, unlike Lear, are wise enough to understand their true nature. Kent takes leave of them by saying—

> And your large speeches may your deeds approve,
> That good effects may spring from words of love!
> (1.1.184-85)

Cordelia truly portrays their character before taking leave of them.

> The jewels of our father, with wash'd eyes
> Cordelia leaves you. I know you what you are;
> And, like a sister, am most loath to call
> Your faults as they are named. (1.1.268-71)

When Goneril rebukes her saying that she has failed to show to her father the obedience which is expected of her, she says that time will reveal what is hidden by false and cunning persons like them and that time begins by concealing faults but at the end reveals them so that persons guilty of those faults have to face shame and ridicule. Soon after grabbing their shares of the kingdom, the two daughters of Lear put their mischievous heads together to conspire and evolve a common strategy to deal with the whims of their father who appears neither affectionate nor generous to these worthless sisters. Immediately after receiving the gifts, they start showing their fangs and prepare to dig them into the weak old man's flesh.

It is Goneril who first speaks of the necessity of doing something to restrain the so called caprices of their father. She opines—

> Pray you, let's hit together: if our father carry authority with such disposition as he bears, this last surrender of his will but offend us. (1.1.302-04)

In this way the conspiracy begins by which the poor king is driven to madness. The simple change from simulated love to actual scorn is clearly seen in the instructions given to Oswald by Goneril—

Put on what weary negligence you please,
You and your fellows; I'ld have it come to question
(1.3.13-14)

and in the determination, thinly veiled by hypocrisy, to cut off the whole of King's train. She does not like the arrangement the King has made for staying, with his hundred knights, with his daughters for one month by turns. But she does not oppose it openly. She conspires and tries to deal with it by her wickedness. She bitterly criticizes his knights saying that they are disorderly, debauched, impudent, gluttonous and lustful. In her criticism, she intentionally distorts and exaggerates the facts. She speaks very harsh words to her father and humiliates him a lot. She sends a letter to Regan, directing her to behave with Lear in the same manner. She directs Oswald—

Inform her full of my particular fear;
And thereto add such reasons of your own
As may compact it more. (1.4.337-39)

Goneril's husband, Albany is a man with a conscience, and his place is by the side of the good persons in this play. He is what he appears to be. At first both the Dukes appear to be alike. But later we find that Albany differs greatly in his character from Cornwall, who fully agrees with his wife Regan with regard to the attitude she adopts towards her father and who himself is as cruel and heartless as Regan and Goneril are. He could not at first understand the treachery of Goneril's heart. When he truly understands her, he strongly condemns her actions. In Act IV Sc. II, he says that the deformity of the fiend is proper to him because it is in keeping with the rest of his being so that the inside and outside agrees with each other. That deformity is less frightful to see than when it appears in a woman's shape because it is unnatural in a woman. He tells her that she is a devil in the shape of a woman. Her real self is devilish but this evil self is covered by a woman's shape. He rightly understands the difference of appearance and reality in her character. He says that she is a monster so far as her nature is concerned and that there is now a danger that in appearance also she will begin to look like a monster. She should not make herself look like the monster which she is. If it had been proper for him to allow his hands to obey the dictates of his mood, he would be ready to break her bones and tear her flesh to make her outward appearance conform to her perverted real self. But he would not like to attack a woman even though the devil dwells inside her. In Act V, Sc. III, Albany says that Goneril is superficially beautiful but is actually dangerous like a snake. To Goneril, he also says—

> Wisdom and goodness to the vile seem vile;
> Filths savour but themselves. What have you done?
> Tigers, not daughters, what have you perform'd?
> (4.2.38-40)

Goneril, in turn, wrongly describes Albany's character. He is not what she says of him—

> Milk-liver'd man!
> That bear'st a cheek for blows, a head for wrongs;
> Who hast not in thy brows on eye discerning.
> Thine honour from thy suffering; (4.2.50-53)

Regan is as much of a hypocrite as Goneril and her professions of love for her father are utterly false. When Lear arrives at the castle, she and her husband at first refuse to meet him on the ground that they are tired of their journey and are feeling unwell. When she meets him after some time, and he complains of the rude behaviour of Goneril, she begins to defend Goneril. She says that she cannot believe that her sister can fail to perform her filial duty. If she has controlled the rowdy behaviour of Lear's knights, she might have done it with some excellent purpose in mind and that she stands free from all blame. When she advises Lear to return to Goneril and seek her forgiveness, he argues against such an unnatural dependence. Regan is such a stone-hearted fellow that when Lear becomes very emotional in his speech—

> Ask her forgiveness?
> Do you but mark how this becomes the house:
> Dear daughter, I confess that I am old;
> Age is unnecessary; on my knees I beg
> That you'll vouchsafe me raiment, bed, and food.
> (2.4.150-54)

she says that he is adopting unseemly tricks to press his point. Though Regan appears to have a gentler and more attractive a countenance than the more resolute Goneril, she delights in cruelty for cruelty's sake. While Goneril suggests the pulling out of Gloucester's eyes, Regan is present at the act itself, plucking the beard of old Gloucester and encouraging her husband in his evil acts. She does not forget to tell Gloucester that his own son, Edmund has revealed his treacherous activities to her and her husband. It is this disclosure by Regan which makes Gloucester realize the blunder he had committed in accepting every word spoken by Edmund as true and in having suspected Edgar of wanting to murder him. It appears at first that Goneril and Regan are faithful towards their husbands. But this is not true. Very soon, it becomes clear that both of them have no place in their hearts for their husbands. Both of them conspire with Edmund and carry on immoral amorous affairs behind the backs of their husbands. Goneril goes to the extent of conspiring to murder her husband in order to win Edmund. Poor Cornwall dies with the impression that his wife loves him a lot. He could not, till his last time, know the real faithlessness of Regan's heart which is hidden behind a fair appearance. It's very late that Albany comes to know about the affair of Goneril with Edmund. He says to Regan in a mocking tone—

> For your claim, fair sister,
> I bar it in the interest of my wife;
> 'Tis she is sub-contracted to this lord,
> And I, her husband, contradict your banns.
> If you will marry, make your loves to me—
> My lady is bespoke. (5.3.85-90)

Albany has now clearly understood the true nature of both the sisters. He does not really mean it when he says that Regan should offer her love to him. He simply makes fun of Regan and Goneril. It appears in the beginning that the two sisters at least love each other. But this also comes out to be false. They are together in all their evil acts. But when the question of Edmund arises, the true character of these sisters is reflected. Both of them want to win Edmund. Their immoral relationship with Edmund leads to a fierce rivalry between the two which finally results in the unnatural deaths of Goneril through suicide and Regan through poison administered by Goneril.

Cordelia is a lady of great truth, honesty and plainness, unlike her two elder sisters. Her love for her father is deep and pure, but it is silent and retiring. Her part is, as she says in the very first words she utters, to 'Love and be silent'. Feminine simplicity, a natural shyness, modesty, an honesty of temperament and an inborn love of truth hold her tongue tied in the opening scene of the play. After hearing the extravagant expression of love from her sisters for their father, she speaks to herself privately—

> Then poor Cordelia!
> And yet not so; since I am sure my love's
> More ponderous than my tongue. (1.1.76-78)

She fully understands her own position and the characters of those with whom she is brought into contact. She can rapidly penetrate motives. She refuses to permit herself to be harmed by Lear's exaggerated passion, and insists on making known to France, the true cause of her father's displeasure. She points out that she has incurred Lear's wrath only because she is lacking in the 'glib and oily art' of flattery, and not because she is guilty of any unchaste action, any dishonourable step, or the crime of murder. The only problem with her is that she does not have a tongue which can utter extravagant words and phrases to praise anybody. In this way, she puts her nature in the right perspective before the king of France. She estimates Duke of Burgundy at a glance, and dismisses him with undisguised contempt. She seems anxious to show her sisters the scorn she feels for them. Her truthfulness and sense of duty are praiseworthy.

> Since what I well intend
> I'll do before I speak— (1.1.225-26)

This is her own simple description of her truthfulness.

Cordelia regards the hypocritical protestations of Goneril and Regan with such contempt that she cannot bring herself to seem like them even in the smallest degree. Through the sincerity of her character, she prefers to submit to be misunderstood, when the exercise of a little tact might have made things all right. Her soundness of judgment is seen in the fact that she sees through the hypocrisy of her sisters. She recognizes the hollowness of the prosperity that comes through hypocrisy. She is glad not to have 'such a tongue', as her sisters have. She wishes her father at some other place—

> But yet, alas, stood I within his grace,
> I would prefer him to a better place. (1.1.273-74)

She understands the sterling worth of Kent—

> O thou good Kent, how shall I live and work,
> To match thy goodness ? (4.7.1-2)

Kent in turn, truly appreciates her—

> The gods to their dear shelter take thee, maid,
> That justly think'st, and hast most rightly said !
> (1.1.182-83)

The King of France is wise enough to understand the real worth of Cordelia. He loves her for her beauty of soul, and not for her physical charms or for her dowry. He defends Cordelia saying that some persons are by nature reserved and reticent and that persons of this nature often omit giving expression to their inner thoughts which actually they intend to put into effect.

Cordelia lacks in demonstration when, as in the first Act, a public display of her affection is demanded. When, however, her father is restored to her after his barbarous experiences at the hands of her sisters, we find a lively, touching demonstration of love from her. When Lear says—

> Be your tears wet? Yes, faith.
> I pray weep not;
> If you have poison for me I will drink it.
> I know you do not love me; for your sisters
> Have, as I do remember, done me wrong;
> You have some cause, they had not. (4.7.69-74)

her reply is as brief as emphatic—

> No cause, no cause. (4.7.75)

Even though treated with so much scorn and injustice by her father she, not even for a moment, harbours any harsh feeling for him. She is, every moment, concerned about his old and whimsical father. When she goes to France, she keeps in touch to get information about her father and returns to England only for the sake of the King's welfare—she has no territorial ambitions against her country. Her truthfulness and honesty and her love for her father stands in sharp contrast with the plaited cunningness of her sisters.

Edmund is gifted with a penetrating insight. He truly understands the nature of his brother and his father and proceeds to build his schemes on these habits—

> A credulous father! and a brother noble,
> Whose nature is so far from doing harms
> That he suspects none; on whose foolish honesty
> My practices ride easy! I see the business.
> Let me, if not by birth, have lands by wit:
> All with me's meet that I can fashion fit. (1.2.170-75)

He knows that his father is superstitious and fully exploits this weakness. He cunningly makes Edgar appear to be what he is not and Gloucester accepts the illusion instead of the reality. In pursuance of his plan to acquire his father's property, he devises a method by which he can prejudice his father against his brother Edgar and by which he can create a complete rift between Edgar and his father. As per his plan, he forges a letter by which he is able to convince his father that Edgar is plotting against Gloucester's life. In order to make Gloucester believe his words, he pretends to be very natural and innocent. He says—

> It is his hand, my lord;
> but I hope his heart is not in the contents. (1.2.64-65)

He plays a double game. On one side, he poisons Gloucester's ears against Edgar and on the other side he wrongly portrays Gloucester before Edgar. When Edgar comes before him, he assures him that he is the well-wisher of Edgar. Whatever he is saying about their father is true. He says—

> Brother, I advise you to the best. I am no honest man if there be any good meaning toward you. I have told you what I have seen and heard; but faintly, nothing like the image and horror of it; (1.2.163-66)

In order to make Gloucester believe in the treachery of Edgar, Edmund cunningly misguides Edgar when he hears his father approaching. He asks Edgar to pretend as if Edmund is fighting with him and he is trying to defend himself. He shouts—

> Yield; come before my father.
> Light, ho, here !—
> Fly, brother.—Torches, torches !—So, farewell.
> (2.1.31-33)

In the meantime he asks Edgar to run away. He deliberately wounds himself so that people would think that he had a desperate fight. Then he gives a fictitious account to Gloucester of the reason why he had fought with Edgar. He says that Edgar had come to murder his father and he was trying to stop him in carrying out his evil designs. At this time he speaks a heap of lies to fill the heart of Gloucester with deep hatred for Edgar. Edmund is such a villain that he has no love and sympathy for his old father. Gloucester thinks that Edmund loves him the most, but the poor fellow could never think, even in his dream, that his son can be so much cruel. He betrays his father to his enemies. It is he who informs Regan and Cornwall about the inclination and activities of Gloucester in taking the side of King Lear. He is responsible for the cruelty done to Gloucester. He is responsible for the sad end of Cordelia and Lear. He makes a plan to have Cordelia murdered in a way so that others may think that she has committed suicide. He instructs his officer to manage the affair in such a way that it should appear to be a suicide case. When Albany enquires about Lear and Cordelia, he again tells lies to deceive him. When he is about to die moral sense and wisdom comes to him. As he lies dying, he says—

> Some good I mean to do
> Despite of mine own nature. (5.3.243-44)

He informs Albany about what he has ordered for Cordelia and Lear. His intention for once is good, but it's too late now. His cruel order has been carried out and he dies with the guilt of his last heartbreaking crime upon him.

With great penetration, Edmund analyses the situation created by Regan and Goneril falling in love with him. He gives a promise of marriage to both of them. He makes amorous relations with both the sisters and pretends to be honest with each of them. Even the wicked sisters are misled by his fair appearance. He has a handsome appearance but a treacherous heart. His every soliloquy is a manifesto of his vicious campaign ruthlessly waged against his poor father & his brother Edgar. Before Edgar comes to meet him for the first time, he prepares himself to put on a sad expression on his face—

> My cue is villainous melancholy, with a sigh like Tom
> O'Bedlam-O, these eclipses do portend these divisions !
> fa, sol, la, mi. (1.2.129-31)

In another soliloquy he says that his brother Edgar has such a noble nature that he can never think of doing any harm to anybody and that he cannot suspect any harm to him from anybody. Because of this nature of Edgar, his intrigues can make a speedy progress. Just like Lear, who is the victim of his daughters' treachery, Gloucester is the victim of his illegitimate son Edmund. The main reason for his acute sufferings is his weakness to judge human characters. He is unable to distinguish between what is real and what appears to be real. He unsuspectingly believes whatever Edmund tells him about Edgar. He takes the contents of the forged letter on their face value and jumps to the conclusion that Edgar has really plotted against his life. He again mistakes appearance for reality when Edmund stages a mock-fight with Edgar. He is disillusioned with the fictitious account given by Edmund about the incident. He thinks Edgar to be his enemy, and Edmund to be very much devoted to him. He puts blind faith in Edmund's story, without trying to summon Edgar to his presence and without questioning him on the subject.

Gloucester asks Edmund to pretend loyalty before Regan and Cornwall. He says that he will secretly go to search and help King Lear and Edmund should speak words of loyalty to Regan and Cornwall so that they could not detect his activities. He says—

> I will look him, and privily relieve him;
> Go you and maintain talk with the Duke, that my charity
> be not of him perceiv'd;
> If he ask for me, I am ill and gone to bed. (3.3.14-17)

As in the case of Lear, knowledge dawns on him only when it is too late to be of any use to him. He repents—

> I have no way, and therefore want no eyes,
> I stumbled when I saw: full of 'tis seen,
> Our means secure us, and our mere defects
> Prove our commodities. (4.1.19-22)

In his utter distress he says that it would be better if he goes mad like Lear so that he may forget his pains by entering into the illusions of insanity. Gloucester is just as credulous and easily deceived as ever, when Edgar fools him about the cliffs of Dover. Having been blinded by the Duke of Cornwall and Regan, Gloucester has made up his mind to commit suicide because the world has become dark for him. He asks a Bedlam-beggar, who is no other than his son Edgar in disguise, to lead him to the top of a cliff at Dover in order that he might jump down from the cliff to die. Edgar brings him into the countryside near Dover and tricks him into believing that he is now standing on the top of a cliff. He jumps down but is not in the least hurt. He is assured by Edgar that he has actually jumped down from a cliff. Edgar now speaks in a different voice thus, pretending that he is not the same man who had led him to the cliff but a different man who was standing on the beach below the cliff.

Edgar and Kent in their disguised forms appear to be what they are not in reality. Edgar is as credulous as his father and believes whatever Edmund tells him. He is deceived by the false appearance of Edmund as well as his father Gloucester. In a soliloquy (Act II, Sc. III), he tells himself that having been proclaimed an outlaw, the only way in which he can save his life is to disguise himself as a Bedlam-beggar. He decides to give himself the name of Tom and from now onwards till almost the end of the play continues in the disguise of a Bedlam-beggar. As a Bedlam-beggar, his madness is feigned and not real. In order to maintain his disguise, he says that he is being chased by the 'foul fiend'. He goes on to describe his sufferings through the foul fiend. He asks Lear, Fool and Kent to beware of the fiend. He tells the Fool that the Fool's singing is that of a demon disguised as a nightingale. He says that the grey cat which is actually a demon in disguise is known by the name of Purr. He, in his mad utterances, advises them to obey their parents, keep their words, not to swear and not to do adultery. Lear, in fact, thinks that he has gone mad because of the ill treatment of his daughters. When Gloucester comes before him, searching for Lear, he continues with his feigned madness. Gloucester is also convinced that he is really mad.

In one of his soliloquies, Edgar thinks about revealing his true identity and throwing off his disguise. He says that now the false story about him has proved to be wrong and he is found to be fair and just. Now he should come to his true position. He has no ill-will towards his father and is very sad to see his miserable condition. In order to fulfill the wishes of his father, he leads him to Dover. He tricks him into believing that he is standing on the top of a cliff. He describes a fictitious picture of the scene from the hill-top and says that one feels terribly frightened and dizzy to look downward from such a great height. He says—

> I'll look no more;
> Lest my brain turn, and the deficient sight
> Topple down headlong. (4.6.22-24)

When Gloucester throws himself forward and falls on the ground, Edgar speaks to himself that a man's imagination or an illusion in his mind can bring about his death if he no longer desires to live. He tricks Gloucester to believe that he has fallen from a great height but has been saved by a miracle. Thus, Edgar does not permit him to commit suicide. He does all this to cure him of his despair.

In his disguised form, Edgar carries to Albany the letter he has discovered from Oswald. In order to prove the charge against Edmund, he fights with him. At this moment, at Edmund's request, he reveals his true identity as Edgar.

Edgar's virtues at the beginning of the play seem to be negative and colourless. He appears to be a credulous, tactless, frightful and cowardly man who tamely does whatever Edmund asks him to do. But as the play advances, it is seen that he is not a tactless and cowardly person. He shows considerable resourcefulness in assuming, successfully, the part first of a mad beggar then of a simple peasant and lastly of a brave strange knight whom even Edmund fails to recognize and who slays down Edmund in a dual.

The Earl of Kent is the very embodiment of loyalty and devotion. In the opening scene, he appears to be rude and unmannerly towards the King. Lear even calls him 'a disloyal courtier'. But this is a wrong judgment of his character. His loyalty and faithfulness for the King and the state knows no limits. Despite the acrimonious treatment he has received from his master, his devotion to him is unswerving and untiring, regardless of the misfortunes he may bring upon himself. In his disguise he follows his enemy King and does him 'service improper for a slave'.

Kent is a plain, blunt and straightforward man. He is not a flatterer or a sycophant to agree with the King no matter what the King says. He does not keep quiet when he sees that such a powerful king, Lear is yielding to flattery (Act I, Sc. I). He truly judges the characters of Goneril, Regan and Cordelia. To Lear, he advises that those who speak in a low voice are not devoid of love and affection. It is the hollow and insincere persons who use high sounding words and phrases to please others. In Act II, Sc. II, Duke of Cornwall says that Kent is a fellow who, having been praised for his plain speaking by someone, now poses to be blunt and rude in his manner of speaking and who twists the habit of plain speaking from its true nature, and turns it towards deception. Such type of persons under the garb of plain speaking, become highly offensive and coarse in their speech. But this is also a wrong estimate of Kent's character. He changes his appearance when he disguises himself, though the reality remains the same. About his disguised form he says—

> If but as well I other accents borrow,
> That can my speech defuse, my good intent
> May carry through itself to that full issue
> For which I raz'd my likeness. (1.4.1-4)

Some of Kent's other speeches also reflect the theme of appearance and reality. To Lear, he says—

I do profess to be no less than I seem;
to serve him truly that will put me in trust; (1.4.12-13)

About Oswald he says that a slave like him carries a sword which is a sign of manhood, yet he lacks an honorable character. Such persons promote every passion in the natures of their masters by their flattery. They deny and affirm just as the moods of their lords require. Such fellows are like dogs which follow their masters blindly. He says that Oswald's face is trying to show a smile while at the same time it is twitching with fear. In one of his speeches he describes about the false servants of the Duke of Albany and Cornwall. He says that both the Dukes have servants who seem to be real servants but who are actually spies and observers, collecting political information about their country and passing it on to the King of France. He again refers to the theme of appearance and reality when he says to the Gentleman—

For confirmation that I am much more
Than my out-wall, open this purse, and take
What it contains. (3.1.44-46)

To Cordelia, Kent begs to adopt the attitude of non-recognition till he finds right time to reveal his true identity (Act IV, Sc. VII). His last words—

I have a journey, sir, shortly to go.
My master calls me, I must not say no. (5.3.321-22)

probably mean that he would soon die out of grief for Lear, though they literally only mean that his master is bidding him to undertake a journey soon, and he should not say no.

The character of Fool in this play is also important. He again and again advocates the use of appearance to conceal reality—

Have more than thou showest,
Speak less than thou knowest,
Lend less than thou owest... (1.4.117-19)

The part of Fool differs from any of his predecessors in the comedies. The clowns of the comedies are introduced mainly to heighten the fun, and their roles are rarely essential to the action. But the Fool in this play is essentially necessary to the action. He brings tragic relief in the play by his wit and humour. He becomes the King's conscience by reminding him of his folly. His role is also of a comforter and helper to him. Because of the tinge of madness in him, he sometimes helps to enhance the pathos in an effort to relieve the tragedy. Lear tries to hide the truth from himself. Fool bitterly reminds him of the truth. The mixture of bitterness, shrewdness and drollery makes his remarks extremely interesting and important rather than merely amusing. The laughter created by him is mortal. His comments inform us about the deeper developments of the play. His actions represent the increasing derangement of Lear's mind. His words echo Lear's own realization of his foolish actions. His last words "And I'll to bed at noon" seems to be pure fooling but express the triumph in Lear of illusion over reality.

4
Othello

Both the internal and external evidences indicate that the play *Othello* must have been composed about the year 1604. The main source of the story of *Othello* is *The Hecatommithi* (Hundred Tales) of Giraldi Cinthio, an Italian novelist.

It is said that *Othello* is a 'tragedy of intrigue'. In this play, a single person Iago plans and executes the intrigues. In fact, the theme of the play can be described as a set of plots and intrigues of Iago to defeat and destroy whoever comes in his way of selfish ambition. The intrigues of Iago against Roderigo, against the place and life of Cassio, against the love of Othello and Desdemona form the main threads with which the tragic lot of *Othello* is woven. *Othello* is also seen as a 'tragedy of misunderstanding'. Othello misunderstands Desdemona and doubts her. He misunderstands Iago and thus, trusts him. Desdemona could not truly understand the depth of Moor's love for her. She could not realize that any threat to this love would lead to the destruction of both of them. Emilia could not understand the evil in the nature of her husband, Iago. Otherwise, she would not give him the handkerchief of Desdemona and the tragedy would be averted. Iago is a coarse and emotionless person. He understands only the physical aspect of love and not the nature of true love which is a matter of soul. He underestimates the power of true love. In an effort to destroy this love, he himself is destroyed along with Othello and Desdemona.

The first lesson that comes up to the surface is that the inability to differentiate truth from falsehood and deceit is a recipe for disaster. Like all the other tragedies of Shakespeare, the fall of the hero of this play occurs mainly because he cannot distinguish what is real from what is illusion. The second lesson implicit in this theme is that evil is not honest about its own nature and always seeks to disguise itself. Iago is not honest to himself, not to talk of others.

The story of *Othello* is nothing if it is not the story of Iago's scheming and plotting against Othello and others. He is the most villainous villain among all the villains of Shakespeare and succeeds in his inhuman villainy because he is an expert, ideal actor. Stephen Greenblatt in his critical essay 'Improvisation of Power' explores the relations of power in a given culture. It brings out the composition of power in Venetian society. Right from the beginning of the play Shakespeare keeps emphasizing the improvised nature of the villain's plot. Iago act as ambiguous third person "to abuse Othello's ear/ That he (Cassio) is to familiar with his wife" (1.3.386-87). This ambiguity is felicitous though not so visible at this point but will be clearly visible later on when he goes ahead with his malicious and outrageous desire for revenge upon Othello's buried perception of his own sexual relations with Desdemona as adulterous. Even though Iago works under the Moor, yet his marks of impromptu or perhaps, his readiness clearly provides him a higher position to his 'master'. Iago is shown to be fully aware of himself as an improviser and revels in his ability to manipulate his victims, to lead them by the nose like assess referring to the fact how he uses their weaknesses against them. Such is the relation Iago establishes with virtually every character in the play, from Othello and Desdemona to minor figures like Roderigo and Bianca. Iago's attitude towards Othello is colonial and he regards his black general as 'an erring barbarian' whose 'free and open nature' is a fertile field for exploitation. Iago conceals his malicious motives towards 'the thick-lips' behind the mask of dutiful service and hence prolongs his improvisation. Iago ultimately destroys all the people he exploits ensuring their defeat. Even though he has no evidence of Desdemona's practice of adultery, his fantastical lies convince Roderigo and Othello. The whole plot is produced through his fantasy. He is able to construct a narrative into which he inscribes those around him.

He acts the part of a friend and well-wisher of Othello and others so well that they are convinced that he is so. He is actually an enemy in the disguise of a friend. He wins the confidence of others by taking interest in their affairs, by giving them sincere advice. Everyone calls him 'honest, honest Iago'. He harms almost every character in the play directly or indirectly but is successful in getting their good opinion and thanks. About him Cassio says—

> I never knew a Florentine more kind and honest. (1.3.40)

Othello says to him from the core of his heart—

> I am bound to thee for ever. (3.3.217)

Desdemona also trusts him when she is in trouble—

> O, god ! Iago,
> What shall I do to win my lord again?
> Good friend, go to him; (4.2.149-51)

These poor honest people could not see his real devilish heart. If we put ourselves in the place of his poor victims, we will also be impressed by his goodness and honesty. It is we, the audience and the readers, who know more about him than the characters in the play know. That is why his honesty is incredible to us but credible to the characters in the play. When we read his soliloquies, we have a glimpse into the working of his devilish mind. He is not actually interested in the case of Roderigo. All the time, he befools Roderigo by speaking in his favour and by promising to help him. He very cunningly draws money from him and uses him for his own purposes.

> Thus do I ever make my fool my purse;
> For I mine own gained knowledge should profane
> If I would time expend with such a snipe
> But for my sport and profit. (1.3.377-80)

So long as Roderigo is of any use to him, he flatters him. But when he finds him standing in his way, he is cruel enough to kill him. To Roderigo, he himself describes his hypocritical nature and illusory loyalty for Othello—

> Were I the Moor, I would not be Iago.
> In following him I follow but myself—
> Heaven is my judge, not I for love and duty,
> But seeming so for my peculiar end.
> For when my outward action doth demonstrate
> The native act and figure of my heart.
> In compliment extern, 'tis not long after
> But I will wear my heart upon my sleeve
> For daws to peck at; I am not what I am. (1.1.54-62)

He advises Roderigo to assume a false appearance in order to deceive others—

> defeat thy favour with an usurped beard. (1.1.339)

Roderigo is misled by Iago because of his hopeless passion for Desdemona. With his cunningness, Iago makes Roderigo believe that Desdemona's love for Othello is false. He presents a fictitious picture of Desdemona before him, who in reality, is innocent and pure. When Roderigo says that she is perfectly chaste, he says—

> Blest fig's end ! The wine she drinks is made of grapes. If she had been blest, she would never have lov'd the Moor. Blest pudding !
>
> Didst thou not see her paddle with the palm of his (Cassios) hand? (2.1.246-49)

He says that Desdemona loved the Moor only because he boasted a lot and told her absurd stories about his bravery. She no longer loves him and Cassio stands the best chance of winning her love in this situation—

> Who stands so eminent in the degree of this fortune as Cassio does? a knave very voluble, no
> further conscionable than in putting on the mere form of civil and humane seeming for the better compass
> of his salt and most hidden loose affection. (2.1.233-37)

In this way he incites Rederigo against Cassio. Roderigo is credulous enough to believe in whatever Iago says and in this way becomes a tool in the hands of Iago. He allows Iago to extort money from him. He does not have the penetrating vision of Iago and fails to see through his duplicity. It's only once in his life that he suspects the wickedness of Iago—

> Every day thou daff'st me with some device,
> Iago; and rather, as it seems to me now, keep'st from
> me all conveniency than suppliest me with the least
> advantage of hope. I will indeed, no longer endure it;
> Nor am I yet persuaded to put up in peace what already I
> have foolishly suffer'd. (4.2.176-81)

He complains that Iago is not acting honestly with him and that he is making a fool of him in this affair. But Iago cools him down by his sweet words. Once again he forgets all about his anger and suspicion against Iago and begins to play in his hand. It's at his last moment that he realizes his foolishness in trusting Iago. But it's too late for him to take revenge.

Outwardly, Iago gives the impression of loyalty, honesty and faithfulness, while inwardly he is disloyal, dishonest and faithless. He hates Cassio. He dislikes Othello, Roderigo and Desdemona. But he convinces each one of them by his flattering words. Othello has no reason to doubt his honesty and loyalty because Iago is the first to tell him of Brabantio's rage against him. He is the first to tell him of Cassio's suspected attitude towards Desdemona. Iago's plans against Othello, Desdemona and Cassio are based mainly on his correct understanding of their characters. His schemes are successful because he strikes at their weak points. He knows—

> The Moor is of a free and open nature,
> That thinks men honest that but seem to be so;
> And will as tenderly be led by th' nose
> As asses are. (1.3.390-93)

He knows that Othello is a simple and credulous fellow. In a very crafty manner, he injects the poison of jealousy in the mind of Othello. He does his work slowly but steadily. He moves forward, comes back, and once again moves ahead with a faked demonstration of hesitation and confusion, carefully guarding the psychological effect of his style on the psychology of his victim.

In one of their discourses both Iago and Othello admit that there should be no distinction between the appearance and reality of a person and that man should be what he appears to be—

> **Iago** - Men should be what they seem;
> Or those that be not, would they might seem none.
> **Othello** - Certain, men should be what they seem. (3.3.129-31)

Here, Othello really means what he says. But Iago's speech is wholly artificial. His one of the other speeches is contradictory to this speech—

> When devils will their blackest sins put on
> They do suggest at first with heavenly shows,
> As I do now. (2.3.339-41)

The problem with Othello is that he could not judge that Iago himself is not what he seems to be. About him, he says—

> And for I know thou art full of love and honesty,
> And weigh'st thy words before thou giv'st them breath,
> Therefore these stops of thine affright me the more;
> For such things in a false disloyal knave
> Are tricks of custom; but in a man that's just
> They're close dilations working from the heart
> That passion cannot rule. (3.3.122-28)

This is one of the examples of verbal irony in the play when the speaker could never, even in a dream, think that the person whom he calls lovable and honest is in reality the most dishonest and wicked person in the play. Iago knows very well that Desdemona is pure, chaste, honest and innocent. But he is a liar both to himself and to others. He deceives himself by false assumptions and does not hesitate in telling lies to Othello. To himself, at least, he cannot deny that Othello's love for Desdemona is true—

> The Moor, howbeit that I endure him not,
> Is of a constant, loving, noble nature;
> And I dare think, he will prove to Desdemona
> A most dear husband. (2.1.282-85)

He knows very well that Desdemona's love for Othello is also deep and genuine. But he feels no pity in slandering an innocent lady like Desdemona. Though chaste in reality she is made to appear unchaste by Iago. He conspires against the happiness and even the lives of Othello, Desdemona and Cassio. He tries to provoke Othello by saying that Desdemona's love for him is not pure—

> And when she seem'd to shake and fear your looks,
> She lov'd them most. (3.3.211-12)

There must be some point in the fact that she rejected several offers of marriage from those of her own country, race, colour and social status, which should have attracted her. Her choice in this matter appears to be vicious and unnatural and she may repent of her marriage with Othello. Iago also says that she pretended to love her father very much but in a moment she broke her relations with him when she eloped with the Moor. She is too young, but she knew how to keep her father completely ignorant of her love affair. That's why her father thought that she could only be won by magic. If she can cheat her own father, how can she be faithful towards him.

At first, Othello could not believe in the words of Iago. But the expressions on his face make Othello suspicious about Desdemona—

> This honest creature doubtless,
> Sees and knows more—much more than he unfolds. (3.3.246-47)

In this state of mental disturbance, he prefers illusion to reality. He says that if a man is robbed it's better that he should not know this. If he does not miss what is stolen, he is not robbed at all. He realizes that he was very happy when he did not know about Desdemona's faithlessness. Now, when he has known the reality, it's very difficult to accept it. He would have been in his peace of mind if he had been living in a world of illusion—

> I saw't not, thought it not, it harm'd not me.
> I slept the next night well, fed well, was free and merry;
> I found not Cassio's kisses on her lips

He that is robb'd, not wanting what is stol'n,
Let him not know't, and he's not robb'd at all.
(3.3.343-347)

Iago gives many arguments to prove his point. He narrates a cunningly fabricated story to Othello that once he lay with Cassio and heard him talking about Desdemona. He weaves the story so well that Othello believes every word of it. In this way, he drags Cassio in between Othello and Desdemona and makes the credulous Moor more than half convinced that Desdemona is false to him. Emilia passes Desdemona's handkerchief to Iago without the remotest suspicion of the villainous game Iago is playing. This handkerchief is a trump card in the hands of Iago and he drops it in the chamber of Cassio. He knows—

Trifles light as air
Are to the jealous confirmations strong
As proofs of holy writ; this may do something.
The Moor already changes with my poison.
Dangerous conceits are in their natures poisons,
Which at the first are scarce found to distaste
But, with a little act upon the blood,
Burn like the mines of sulphur. (3.3.326-33)

When Iago next meets Othello, he is in a state of great mental perturbation. At this stage, Iago informs Othello that his wife has given the handkerchief, which he had given to her as a token of his love, to Cassio. In order to confirm his suspicion, he asks Othello to demand that handkerchief from Desdemona. When demanded, Desdemona could not produce that handkerchief. Othello's suspicions about his wife are intensified. He asks Iago to give him a proof of Desdemona's unfaithfulness. According to the plan of Iago, Othello stands at a distance to see how Cassio talks about Desdemona. Iago excites Cassio to talk about Bianca, a prostitute who loves him. On hearing the name of Bianca, Cassio jeers and laughs at her. Othello misinterprets the jeering and gestures of Cassio and thinks that they all refer to Desdemona. At this time Bianca appears and Othello sees Desdemona's handkerchief in her hand. He is greatly inflamed against Desdemona because he thinks that she has given the handkerchief to Cassio, and the latter to Bianca. Thus one after another misunderstandings make Othello mad and blind by rage. He resolves to kill Desdemona. The next time, when he meets her, he slanders and abuses her openly and does not give her any chance to prove her innocence. He considers her weeping artificial—

> O devil, devil !
> If that the earth could teem with woman's tears,
> Each drop she falls would prove a crocodile,
> Out of my sight ! (4.1.240-43)

To Lodvico, Othello says that Desdemona is not a virtuous woman. She can change her loyalty and yet go on playing a virtuous woman. She is a fine picture of grief. Her entire weeping is artificial. To Desdemona, he says that she resembles a heavenly creature, but she is a devil in reality. He also rebukes her saying—

> Was this fair paper, this most goodly book,
> Made to write 'whore' upon? (4.2.72-73)

When Desdemona says that she is chaste and true to him, he rebukes her saying that she is as true in quick breeding as the flies in a mutton market on a hot day where they begin to breed as soon as they come out of eggs. She is a wild poisonous flower which is lovely to look at and has a killing fragrance. When Othello finally decides to murder Desdemona, he is under wrong impression that he is committing a crime to redeem his honour and thus is an 'honourable murderer'. He justifies his proposed action, for—

> She must die, else she'll betray more men. (5.2.6)

Just before her death, when Desdemona comes to know about the reason for Othello's anger, she requests him to send for Cassio and enquire from him the truth. Othello thinks that Cassio must be dead. When he tells Desdemona about the death of Cassio, she suddenly broke out—

> O, my fear interprets ! What, is he dead? (5.2.77)

and

> Alas, he is betray'd, and I undone! (5.2.80)

Actually, by saying this Desdemona means that now there is no one to prove her innocence. She simply pities the death of honest Cassio and is afraid of her own fate. But once again Othello misunderstands her. He believes that these words of Desdemona are an expression of her deep concern and love for Cassio. She is weeping just because her lover has died. In a state of blind fury, he stabs Desdemona. When Emilia exposes the villainy of Iago and tells him the real facts regarding the disappearance of the handkerchief, he realizes the mistake he has made. Deeply troubled by his guilty conscience for having killed his innocent wife on the basis of false suggestions made by Iago, Othello commits suicide. In his last speech, he characterises himself as—

> Of one that lov'd not wisely, but too well;
> Of one not easily jealous, but, being wrought,
> Perplexed in the extreme; of one whose hand,
> Like the base Indian, threw a pearl away
> Richer than all his tribe; of one whose subdued eyes,
> Albeit unused to the melting mood,
> Drops tears as fast as the Arabian trees
> Their medicinable gum. (5.2.347-54)

Thus, *Othello* is a tragedy in which a husband commits the murder of his wife under the mistaken impression that she is playing false to him and she is unchaste. Just as Othello wrongly estimates Desdemona, Desdemona's estimate of Othello's character comes out to be wrong. When she loses her handkerchief, she says to Emilia—

> Believe me, I had rather lose my purse
> Full of crusadoes; and but my noble Moor
> Is true of mind, and made of no such baseness
> As jealous creatures are, it were enough
> To put him to ill thinking. (3.4.22-26)

She has strong faith in her husband's loyalty, honesty and balance of temperament. According to her, Othello is a man of strong character and firm determination. He can never be infected by lower instincts like jealousy, malice and hatred—

> I think the sun where he was born
> Drew all such humours from him. (3.4.27-28)

When Othello behaves with her in a strange manner, she could not understand the reason for his annoyance. She thinks that some serious news from Venice, or the discovery of some conspiracy in Cyprus must have shocked him. Men are likely to be disturbed with small things when they are obsessed with more serious affairs. This must be the case with Othello. His mind must be obsessed with some problem related to the state and thus, very small thing like the loss of handkerchief has upset him. But she is wrong in her judgment.

The chief cause of the untimely and sad death of Desdemona is her innocence and inability to judge characters. She fails to suspect that some ill feelings against her are working up in her husband's mind. Had Desdemona correctly understood the mood of Othello and guessed the possibility of a plot against herself, she would have saved herself with an immediate explanation. She can never suspect that her husband can be so cruel as to murder her. Her love is so pure that when Othello stabs her mortally and she is about to die, she does not like to accuse him of her murder. She says that she herself has committed the deed. She, like all the other characters in the play, could not opportunity to instill into Othello's mind the poison of jealousy. And the result will be that the more earnestly she pleads for Cassio, the more seriously she will invoke Othello's suspicion—

> I'll pour this pestilence into his ear—
> That she repeals him for her body's lust;
> And by how much she strives to do him good
> She shall undo her credit with the Moor.
> So will I turn her virtue into pitch; (2.3.344-48)

Everything happens as per Iago's plan. The interview between Cassio and Desdemona is cut short by the appearance of Othello and Cassio departs without speaking to Othello. This Cassio does out of fear but Iago seizes upon this point and makes the insinuating remark about Cassio's stealing away 'So guilty-like, seeing you coming.' While talking to Othello, Iago pretends ignorance that Cassio had been acquainted with Desdemona. The way in which Iago says 'indeed' on hearing that Cassio had carried messages during the period of their courtship, strikes

Othello. His hesitation about expressing his opinion about Cassio makes Othello suspicious. Othello expresses absolute trust in the honesty and faithfulness of Iago. Iago now begins to give direct answer to his questions. Before he leaves him, he takes care to direct the suspicion to Cassio. At the demand of Othello, Iago gives him many proofs by inventing false stories. In this way Cassio who is very honest, is made to appear dishonest by Iago. Iago is such a cruel person that he himself gives a deadly wound to Cassio, whom he calls his best friend throughout the play. He does it in such a way that Cassio could not see him. Then, he is so shrewd that he tries to put the responsibility of wounding Cassio on innocent Bianca. He openly declares that Bianca has something to do with the matter. About Bianca, he says—

> Look you pale, mistress?—
> Do you perceive the gastness of her eye?—
> Nay, if you stare, we shall hear more anon—
> Behold her well; I pray you look upon her.
> Do you see gentlemen ? Nay, guiltiness will speak
> Though tongues were out of use. (5.1.103-08)

The theme of appearance and reality is also reflected in Iago's cynical contempt for the virtue of woman. While talking to Desdemona, he speaks ill of women as a class. He says that if a woman is fair and wise, her wisdom knows how to turn her beauty to account. If a woman is black and wise, her wisdom knows how to secure a good husband. A woman, however ugly and foolish, knows how to imitate the vices of the fair and wise one. About women he says—

> You are pictures out a-doors,
> Bells in your parlours, wildcats in your kitchens,
> Saints in your injuries, devils being offended,
> Players in your huswifery, and huswives in your beds.
> (2.1.109-12)

Iago is so much given to suspecting the goodness of others that at last he begins to suspect himself. If there is a jealous husband in *Othello*, it's Iago, not Othello. He does not think that his own wife, Emilia can be true to him. Nor can he believe that Cassio and Othello can be constant and faithful in their love for the lady they love. He also suspects that Cassio and Othello have seduced his wife, Emilia.

Emilia is a faithful maid of Desdemona. She gives away Desdemona's handkerchief to Iago. But she could never think that Iago must be playing such a horrible game. One thing should always be remembered that she does not steal the handkerchief as she is asked by her husband to do, but obtains it by chance. She is simply anxious to please her husband. The relation between Iago and Emilia is not happy. When she gives the handkerchief to Iago, she expects that Iago would be happy with her. She has no intention of injuring her mistress. The point that she remains silent over the matter while there is a misunderstanding between Desdemona and Othello regarding the handkerchief, produces doubt against her. But she could never anticipate the tragic consequence to which the loss of handkerchief would lead. Her impression is that Othello is jealous for some reason or other. She suspects the cause for Othello's jealousy—

> I will be hang'd if some eternal villain.
> Some busy and insinuating rogue,
> Some cogging, cozening slave, to get some office,
> Have not devis'd this slander; I'll be hanged else.
> (4.2.132-35)

At this time, Iago is standing by her, yet Emilia's suspicion never for a moment turns to him. This is an instance of subtle dramatic irony in the play. Never has a woman been more mistaken in her husband. How knave and shrewd Iago is that he succeeds in impressing his wife with his out spoken honesty and bluntness of manner as he does Othello and others. Emilia knows that Iago may not be an ideal husband. He may be foul-tongued. But she never suspects that he would be such a wicked villain as to wreck the peace and happiness of two innocent lovers. She is much amazed when Othello tells her that Iago was his informer. She repeatedly cries 'My husband'. Moreover, she knows nothing of her husband's wickedness and remains quiet to save him. But when the wickedness of Iago is known to her, she does not spare him even at the risk of her own life. Othello misjudges Emilia. When he grows suspicious about Desdemona, he cross-examines Emilia about her mistress. She solemnly swears that Desdemona is virtuous and that she has nothing to do with Cassio. But Othello does not believe her. He thinks that Emilia is a party to the guilty passion between Cassio and Desdemona—

> She says enough; yet she is a simple bawd
> That cannot say as much. This is a subtle whore,
> A closet-lock-and-key of villainous secrets;
> And yet she'll kneel and pray, I have seen her do't.
> (4.2.20-23)

The whole matter becomes clear in the end. Emilia is neither unfaithful to Desdemona and Othello, nor to her husband Iago. She appears to be a shrewd and selfish woman, but actually she is practical and worldly wise.

When Desdemona elopes with her lover Othello, and Iago and Roderigo informs her father Brabantio about her elopement. When Brabantio sees Roderigo, he thinks that he has again came to disturb him by begging Desdemona hand. He scolds him saying that he can never have Desdemona and he should no more disturb his peace. When Iago and Roderigo informs him about Desdemona's elopement, he does not believe it. He thinks that they are trying to insult him by saying this. After hearing the arguments of Iago and Roderigo, he grows suspicious and reflects what he has in his mind—

> This accident is not unlike my dream.
> Belief of it oppresses me already. (1.1.143-44)

Finally, when Brabantio himself finds his daughter missing from the house, he is shocked. He cries out—

> O, thou deceivest me
> Past thought ! (1.1.166-67)

He says that a father should not judge his daughter by her fair appearance only. The daughter who seems to be fair and innocent in appearance, can be very wicked and full of ingratitude. Then, he suspects that his daughter must have done this under the influence of some magical charm—

> O ! treason of the blood !
> Fathers, from hence trust not your daughter's minds

By what you see them act. Is there not charms
By which the property of youth and maidhood
May be abus'd ? (1.1.170-74)

Desdemona chooses Othello in preference to her own people, because she loves the greatness, goodness and nobility of his soul, and not his black body. She sees the grandeur of his mind within the outer black skin of his. This is real and pure love, which pierces beneath appearances and is guided by what is within. The blackness of Othello's body is emphasized in order to highlight the whiteness and nobility of his character and the purity and intensity of Desdemona's love for him. The character of Othello is striking because of his blackness as compared with the rest of the characters in the play who are all white. The characters in the play refer to his blackness but its only Iago, the villain who makes it a point of contempt and ridicule. The Duke correctly estimates his character when he tells Brabantio that his son-in-law is more fair than black—

And, noble signior,
If virtue no delighted beauty lack,
Your son-in-law is far more fair than black. (1.3.288-90)

Shakespeare wants us to use our insight to see Othello as a black man and to appreciate his inner life as a splendid soldier and servant of the state of Venice. His anxiety in the last scene of the play is also in accordance with the theme of appearance and reality. The dying Othello, like dying Hamlet, fears that he might be misunderstood and misjudged by the people after his death. The dying Hamlet requests Horatio to remain alive in order to tell people his story in all its truthfulness. Similarly Othello, just before his death, requests his fellowmen to narrate his story in all its truthfulness—

I have done the state some service, and they know't—
No more of that. I pray you, in your letters,
When you shall these unlucky deeds relate,
Speak of me as I am; nothing extenuate,
Nor set down aught in malice. (5.2.342-46)

5
Antony and Cleopatra

Antony and Cleopatra occupies a definite place among Shakespeare's Roman plays. These plays differ from the great tragedies in as much as the background, the atmosphere and the environment is always provided by the larger political life of the state.

The events of the play cover a period of about ten years from 40 B.C. when the Roman empire was partitioned among the triumvirates—Octavius, Antony and Lepidus—to 30 B.C. when Antony died leaving the vast empire in the lap of Octavius. It is a unique play in the sense that it is a history, a love poem as well as a tragedy. Fact and fiction are most harmoniously brought together in the inventive hands of the master dramatist. On one hand it highlights the political state of the Roman empire, on the other it resembles *Romeo and Juliet* and *Troilus and Cressida* in probing the depths of love. Yet this love is not recklessly passionate and youthful but middle aged. They do not reject the world until it rejects them.

Antony and Cleopatra is also a tragedy although much less intellectual than the other Shakespearean tragedies. There is a greater expansiveness of the characters and thoughts. While the others have a stronger melodramatic element, this play is obviously on a lower key. Nevertheless it is a tragedy of love. The aspect of false appearances can be aptly observed in the theme of the play itself as what appears to be a superficial tale of earthly love is in fact much more. It is accompanied with undercurrents of pathos, degradation, treachery and guilt in a world which is outwardly magnificent but decaying inside. It is a world where every relationship is exploited for one's material gains and loyalties change with the change of fortune.

When Antony receives the news of his wife Fulvia's death, whose death he desires, he appears to be disturbed—

> There's a great spirit gone !
> Thus did I desire it.
> What our contempts doth often hurl from us
> We wish it ours again;....
> ....She's good, being gone;
> The hand could pluck her back that shoved her on.
> (1.2.119-24)

Antony then promptly puts the transient grief aside and prepares to leave for Rome to answer Pompey's challenge. Cleopatra even mocks at him for his lack of compassion—

> O most false love !
> Where be the sacred vials thou shouldst fill
> With sorrowful water ? Now I see, I see
> In Fulvia's death how mine received shall be. (1.3.62-65)

This also goes to prove Antony practical to the point of being cruel in all relations except with Cleopatra.

In *Antony and Cleopatra* Octavius has been introduced as a foil to Antony. Where Antony is rash and self-indulgent, Octavius is cautious and calculating. His extreme sobriety is striking. The fact that highlights our theme of false pretensions is that a clever and calculating politician like Octavius appears to be polite and friendly towards Antony only because he is wary of his might. He resents Antony's lustful revelry in Egypt because he needs him to prove a match against the rebellious Pompey. That Antony is a more formidable rival is justified by Pompey when he confides in Varrius that Antony's knowledge of warfare is twice as great as Octavius and Lepidus. Octavius has this point in mind when he superficially welcomes Antony to Rome and although offended by earlier events, expresses his desire to forget and forgive. He acknowledges the superior soldiership of Antony and this alone leads him to enter into a compromise with Antony, which both break later on. In spite of his strong contempt for Antony, he patches up with him for necessity's sake. In fact, he exploits Antony's rash valour and succeeds in crushing the might of Pompey. Octavius is selfish, cunning and devoid of human warmth. Another event which highlights the dual policy of Octavius is the marriage alliance of his sister Octavia with Antony which is purely utilitarian. He is a subtle and crafty politician who can sacrifice all to gain his political and public ambitions. He pretends to be a loving and caring brother and yet stakes his sister's life, fixing her marriage with Antony for the sake of compromise. In accepting the proposed marriage, he is probably laying a trap for his enemy. He boasts endlessly of his love for his sister but they prove to be hollow sentiments—

> There is my hand.
> A sister I bequeath you, whom no brother
> Did ever love so dearly. Let her live
> To join our kingdoms and our hearts; and never
> Fly off our loves again ! (2.2.153-57)

He catches at Agrippa's suggestion as a drowning man catches at a straw and never once protests in spite of being in full knowledge of Antony's obsession with the Egyptian queen. This marriage is a marriage of convenience and Octavius sacrifices his sister for political ends. Many critics denounce his callous treatment of his sister. Caesar is mean and repulsive—nothing gallant and chivalrous in his treatment of his enemies. As soon as Antony's back is turned, he destroys first Pompey and then Lepidus. He defends himself—

> I have told him Lepidus was grown too cruel,
> That he his high authority abused,
> And did deserve his change. For what I have conquered
> I grant him part; but then, in his Armenia,
> And other of his conquer'd kingdoms, I Demand the like.
> (3.6.32-36)

Later the relations between Antony and Caesar deteriorate. Now he finds pretexts to make war on Antony, since he is the only obstacle to his attainment of world mastery. Octavia's arrival at Rome to make a futile effort to reconcile them gives him this excuse. She comes poorly attended and he concludes that Antony has deliberately sent her to Rome in this manner to insult him—

> Why have you stol'n upon us thus? You come not
> Like Caesar's sister. The wife of Antony
> Should have an army for an usher,... (3.6.42-44)

and

> The ostentation of our love, which left unshown.
> Is often left unloved... (3.6.52-53)

Caesar convinces his sister that she has been wronged by Antony and it is his fraternal responsibility to avenge her humiliation. But the reality is that poor Octavia is deceived by both her husband and her brother. Octavius appears to be protective of his sister's interests—

> Nothing more dear to me. You are abus'd
> Beyond the mark of thought, and the high gods,
> To do you justice, make their ministers
> Of us and those that love you... (3.6.86-89)

In reality he is forwarding his own selfish motive. His astuteness in war is rewarded with success. Although Antony is definitely more gallant and mighty than him but, Caesar's refusal to meet the enemy in a land fight and his ability to take advantage of his enemy's folly shows his tact. His speech on hearing of Antony's death appears to show genuine sorrow. But it is a formal tribute paid by the victor for his own glory.

As Antony dies in Cleopatra's arms, Cleopatra declares to end her life 'after the high Roman fashion'. Caesar pretends to be deeply touched with the news of Antony's death and pays a glowing tribute to him. Cleopatra's messenger arrives in order to know his intentions towards the queen Cleopatra. Octavius shrewd and crafty as he is sends word of comfort to her lest she too, should follow the way of Antony and thus defeat his purpose. He does not want to be deprived of the pleasure of humiliating her by taking her in triumph through Rome. He appears to be sympathetic and compassionate. He sends his own messengers to Cleopatra to convince her with soothing words and an offer of an honourable treatment—

> We purpose her no shame. Give her what comforts
> The quality of her passion shall require,
> Lest, in her greatness, by some mortal stroke
> She do defeat us; for her life in Rome
> Would be eternal in our triumph. (5.1.62-66)

Octavius tries to capture Cleopatra through deception. He appears to be sympathetic and generous towards her thus concealing his real intention of subjecting her to humiliation. At the monument, Proculeius and Gallus, the messengers of Caesar arrive apparently to console Cleopatra that her honour and interests are in the safe hands of Caesar and within seconds Cleopatra is made a prisoner. At this, she suspects that Caesar means to carry her to Rome as a captive. She also tries to kill herself but fails. Now she is resolute not to fall into the hands of Caesar—

> ...Shall they hoist me up,
> And show me to the shouting varletry
> Of censuring Rome ? Rather a ditch in Egypt
> Be gentle grave unto me ! Rather on Nile's mud
> Lay me stark-naked, and let the water-flies
> Blow me into abhorring ! (5.2.55-60)

She asks how Caesar means to treat her and Dolabella confirms her suspicion that Caesar intends to display her as a trophy through the streets of Rome. There starts Cleopatra's last act of deception. She deals with the cold and calculating Octavius in a different way; in fact she gives him a dose of his own medicine. She kneels before him and hails him as—'My master and my Lord.' Caesar offers a subtle threat that if she acts according to his instructions, he would be gentle towards her and if she follows Antony's course, he would get her sons killed—

> If you apply yourself to our intents—
> Which towards you are most gentle-you shall find
> A benefit in his change; but if you seek
> To lay me a cruelty by taking

> Antony's course, you shall bereave yourself
> Of my good purposes, and put your children
> To that destruction which I'll guard you from
> If thereon you rely. (5.2.125-32)

To this Cleopatra promises—

> And may, through all the world. 'Tis yours, and we.
> Your scutcheons and your signs of conquest, shall
> Hang in what place you please. Here, my good lord
> (5.2.133-35)

She puts his mind at rest, convincing him that she has no desire to commit suicide and Octavius goes feeling smug and satisfied. But Cleopatra is not fooled by his assurances and she prepares to carry out her plan of committing suicide. She orders Charmian to bring her robe and crown. The means of her deliverance come to her in the form of asps in a basket full of figs brought by a rustic. She dies defeating the invincible Caesar. She courts death rather than indignation at the hands of Caesar. Octavius is perfect at deceiving but fails this time. Cleopatra has peered into his villainous heart and refuses to fall into his tricky trap. In fact, she tricks him and he is all the time foolishly led to believe that Cleopatra is under his thumb. She deceives the deceiver and his being outwitted puts him in still worse light.

In Cleopatra, Shakespeare has successfully created a glittering warm seductress who is the epitome of mystery, fascinating and fatal charm. He has extolled and glorified the Egyptian queen and given her a rare prominence and greatness, thus lavishing all his artistry on the siren. She has been immortalised in the poetic precision of Enobarbus—

> Age cannot wither her, nor custom stale
> Her infinite variety. Other women cloy
> The appetites they feed; but she makes hungry
> Where most she satisfies; for vilest things.
> Become themselves in her; that the holy priests
> Bless her when she is riggish. (2.2.239-44)

She enchants and bewitches not only Antony, but men like Enobarbus and even Dolabella. Only the hard-hearted Octavius resists her charms. Her forwardness of moods and technique of keeping Antony in her influence are extraordinary. This she does through different acts. She, in reality is quite sensible and capable, yet before Antony, she puts on an act of vulnerability and delicacy of nerves—

> Help me away, dear Charmian ! I shall fall.
> It cannot be thus long; the sides of nature
> Will not sustain it... (1.3.15-17)

When Charmian suggests to her to let Antony have his way, she rebukes her by saying—

> Thou teachest like a fool—the way to lose him. (1.3.10)

But she is aware of the transience of love and is always insecure of Antony's love for her. She is ironic and satirical when he expresses his love for her—

> Excellent falsehood !
> Why did he marry Fulvia, and not love her?
> I'll seem the fool I'm not; Antony
> Will be himself. (1.1.40-43)

When Cleopatra is informed of Antony's imminent departure to Rome she instructs—

> See where he is, who's with him; what he does.
> I did not send you. If you find him sad,
> Say I am dancing; of in mirth, report
> That I am sudden sick. Quick, and return. (1.3.2-5)

She is a mistress of guiles, a queen of treachery. She is upset at Antony's departure but pretends to be cool and wants to make him feel guilty and thus, trap him into submission. She challenges him—

> Why should I think you can be mine and true,
> Though you in swearing shake the throned gods.
> Who have been false to Fulvia? (1.3.27-29)

Even though she is directly responsible for the debacle at Actium, she is able to apologize amply to Antony and appears so repentant and tearful that Antony becomes his former self, protective and indulgent—

> Fall not a tear, I say; one of them rates
> All that is won and lost... (3.11.69-70)

Cleopatra's character is enigmatic and unpredictable for she keeps on behaving in ways opposed to her real self to such extent that her true self cannot be defined for instance her behaviour with Thyreus, Caesar's messenger. When he discloses that Caesar pities her that she did not accept Antony out of love but out of fear, Cleopatra is quick to grasp the opportunity. For Caesar, she says—

> He is a god, and knows
> What is most right. Mine honour was not yielded,
> But conquered merely. (3.13.60-62)

She even allows Thyreus to kiss her hand, an offence for which he is punished to be whipped by Antony. Cleopatra remains to all an enigma, bewitching and fascinating with her shifty illusive colours. Even Enobarbus defends her when Antony says—

> **Ant.** - She is cunning past man's thoughts.
>
> **Eno.** - Alack, sir, no! Her passions are made of nothing but the finest part of pure love. We cannot call her winds and waters, sighs and tears; they are greater storms and tempests than almanacs can report. This cannot be cunning in her; if it be she makes a shower of rain as well as Jove. (1.2.141-46)

Time and again she lets down Antony and makes up things with her quick passions, sensual pleas and startling wit. Her character has always been tinted with suspicion. Despite authentic claims of her everlasting love for Antony, he doubts her frequently. He even accuses her—

> I found you as a morsel cold upon
> Dead Caesar's trencher. Nay, you were a fragment
> Of Cneius Pompey's; besides what hotter hours,
> Unregistered in vulgar fame, you have
> Luxuriously pick'd out: for, I am sure.
> Though you can guess what temperance should be.
> You know not what it is. (3.13.116-22)

To say the least, she is an opportunist led by her passions and instincts. Among Shakespearean characters she is known to be consistently inconsistent. Her name has become a synonym of deception and fickleness. Though she vindicates herself by dying a glorious death rather than giving up her honour, it is again done through clever deceit. She deceives the deceiver Octavius. Countless controversies have raged over the genuineness and artifice in her disposition but all in vain. In her, appearance and reality have blended in such perfect harmony that they cannot be differentiated.

Antony, on the other hand is a victim of appearance discrimination. Though not a shadow of his former glory, he hastens his decline by blunders and needless foolhardiness. He appears to be passive, indecisive and faulty in judgments. He is the seniormost triumvir, the master of one-third of the world. Even the fierce, warlike Parthians yield to the might of this 'demi-atlas of the earth'. His name is enough to strike terror in the hearts of his foes like Pompey. And yet strangely enough he becomes the slave of a seductress. His followers Demetris and Philo resent this degrading infatuation of their master—

Nay, but this dotage of our general's
O'erflows the measure. Those his goodly eyes,
That o'er the files and musters of the war
Have glow'd like plated Mars, now bend, now turn,
The office and devotion of their view
Upon a tawny front. His captain's heart,
Which in the scuffles of great fights hath burst
The buckles of his breast, reneges all temper.
And is become the bellows and the fan
To cool a gipsy's lust. (1.1.1-10)

Millions depend on him for the safety of their life and yet to him kingdoms are clay and he would let Rome melt in Tiber.

On one hand, Antony makes vociferous claims of his unique love for Cleopatra, on the other he reaches Rome and marries Octavia, forgetting Cleopatra and his protestations of love. Thus, he deceives Cleopatra to forward his selfish pleasure seeking ambitions. Maybe he has seen the golden opportunity of inheriting Caesar's throne. Though he marries Octavia for political advantage yet he, in his heart of hearts, is conscious of the fact that he will return to Cleopatra—

I will to Egypt;
And though I make this marriage for my peace,
I'th' East my pleasure lies. (2.3.39-41)

Thus, Antony must be held equally responsible with Caesar for exploiting Octavia, and simultaneously cheating Cleopatra. Soon after his marriage to Octavia he returns to Cleopatra. He allows Octavia to go to Rome and mediate between him and Caesar. Thereafter the deterioration of his character is rapid. It is the beginning of the end. Against his better reason and the sane suggestions of his comrades, he chooses to fight Caesar by sea. And when Cleopatra flees from the battle in terror, he too 'claps on his sea wing like a doting mallard'—a shameful act which leaves irretrievable guilt.

Antony's love for Cleopatra does not inspire and motivate, but degrades and shames him. He swings between love and hatred, frequently suspecting her but as soon as she sheds a few tears, she is pardoned. He pulls himself up from infatuation with a strong will power and yet sinks into it again to his utter ruin and destruction.

Mark Antony is one of the most complex characters of Shakespeare. His nature is composed of opposite traits—courage and frailty, self-restrain and self-indulgence, selfishness and generosity. When he finds Thyreus, Caesar's messenger kissing Cleopatra's hand he is cruel and vindictive and orders his servants to whip him till he cries with pain like a child. He is also furious with Cleopatra. When his rage subsides, the two are reconciled. He again decides to give one last heroic battle to Caesar, and then calls for one more night of revelry. After all this, Enobarbus cannot any more stand his folly and fickle mindedness and decides to go over to Caesar. He leaves his 'chests and treasures' behind him, but Antony orders that his belongings together 'with his bounty overplus' should be sent to him. A man who appeared to be petty and unchivalrous moments ago displays nobility and generosity in reality. This fills Enobarbus with remorse. He is tormented with his guilt and 'dies of thought'.

After his final defeat, Antony is devastated at the Egyptian desertion once again and pours out his soul to Eros—

I made these wars for Egypt, and the Queen
Whose heart I thought I had, for she had mine,
Which, whilst it was mine had annex'd unto't.
A million moe, now lost—she, Eros, has
Pack'd cards with Caesar, and false—play'd my glory
Upon an enemy's triumph. (4.14.15-20)

But as soon as Cleopatra's messenger gives him the false news of Cleopatra's death, he in a flash decides to end his life. He dies in the Egyptian's arms advising her to seek her honour and protection from Caesar. No doubt passion is the force that leads to his destruction, but it is grand and noble all the same, it lifts him to the height of tragic greatness.

Lepidus is the most insignificant of the triumvirs. Caesar treats him with contempt though Antony is habitually courteous to him. He tries to keep up his position by flattering both Antony and Caesar. A glimpse of his character is given in Act III, Sc. II, in the conversation between Agrippa and Enobarbus—

Agr. - 'Tis a noble Lepidus.

Eno. - A very fine one; O'how he loves Caesar !

Agr. - Nay, but how dearly he adores Mark Antony !

....

Agr. - Indeed, he plied them both with excellent praises.

Eno. - But he loves Caesar best. Yet he loves Antony. (3.2.6-15)

Enobarbus points out that Antony and Caesar are the wings that raise this beetle i.e. Lepidus from the ground. Lepidus knows this fact fully and strives to reconciliate them in order to safeguard his own interest. For his selfish motive to remain an integral part of the triumvirate, he is obsequious to both the gallants. He goes out of his way to smoothen the edges at the crucial meeting of the two when Antony reaches Rome in an aggressive mood. The credit for the compromise between them also goes to some extent to Lepidus. At Pompey's galley as he entertains the triumvirs, one of the intelligent servants remarks on the position of Lepidus—

> To be called into a huge sphere, and not to be seen to move in't are the holes where eyes should be, which pitifully disaster the checks. (2.7.14-16)

Lepidus is 'maudlin—and stupid drunk. In fact he allows himself to be ridiculed by Enobarbus and Antony to be in their good books. Still, all his attempts prove to be in vain. Caesar first defeats Pompey with the help of Lepidus, and then deposes and imprisons Lepidus himself.

Pompey also displays contradictions in his character and actions. He is obviously a brilliant soldier, for Caesar is quite wary of him. He succeeds in exploiting the greatness of his father. But he is outwitted by Caesar. In the scene where the agreement is made between him and the triumvirs, he exchanges his real hold over the sea for the illusory guarantee of a paper treaty. His father would never have surrendered his power like this. He makes loud protestations of his preference for justice, yet he takes in his service Menas and Menecrates 'great thieves by the sea'.

During the drunken revelry and wild merriment at Pompey's galley, intrigue and conspiracy are also visible. Menas offers him a murderous proposal to get rid of Antony, Caesar and Lepidus. He whispers a sinister suggestion in his ear; that they should first cut the cables of the ship and then the throats of the triumvirs. In this way, Pompey could become the master of the world. But Pompey turns down the proposal on ground of false honour—

> Ah ! This thou shouldst have done,
> And not have spoke on't. In me 'tis villainy:
> In thee't had been good service. (2.7.72-74)

This exposes the petty intrigues and false concepts of honour in men of standing. Pompey would not betray his guests. He would have approved of the plot had it been executed secretly. While his true self would have loved to get his rivals killed yet he turns down the offer as he is afraid to spoil his reputation. His notions of chivalry and honour are weird, as he refuses to kill his enemies because of his concern for appearances. Though his heart is filled with hatred and vicious dislike for his rivals, yet he would not be remembered for open treachery.

The battle of Actium between Caesar and Antony is a decisive one as it seals the destiny of Antony, when he spinelessly runs away from the battle at sea led by the seductress. Later his conscience torments him and despite Enobarbus' desertion he motivates his men and wins a battle. Octavius modifies his war strategy. He knows that he has little chance against Antony in a fight on land. So he challenges Antony for a sea fight again. Antony divides his forces into two, he himself commanding the land forces, but is devastated when he sees the Egyptian fleet deserting him and going over to Caesar's side. He suspects Cleopatra of treachery and in anger calls her 'a triple turned whore'—

> This foul Egyptian hath betrayed me.
> My fleet hath yielded to the foe; and yonder
> They cast their caps up and carouse together
> Like friends long lost. Triple-turned whore ! 'tis thou
> Hast sold me to this novice; and my heart
> Makes only wars on thee. (4.12.10-15)

He also says—

> O this false soul of Egypt! this grave charm—
> Whose eye beck'd forth my wars, and call'd them home;
> Whose bosom was my crownet, any chief end—
> Like a right gipsy hath at fast and loose
> Beguiled me to the very heart of loss. (4.12.25-29)

Antony pours out his agony to Eros. He is disgusted with the treacherous ways of the world where appearances overshadow the reality. Here Antony's speech is the epitomising definition of deceptive appearances—

> Sometimes we see a cloud that's dragonish;
> A vapour sometime like a bear or lion,
> A tower'd citadel, a pendent rock,
> A forked mountain, or blue promontory
> With trees upon't, that are nod unto the world
> And mock our eyes with air. (4.14.3-8)

To Antony, all such shapes merely delude the world with their unreal appearances. He has Cleopatra and Enobarbus in his mind whom he had trusted absolutely. He says to Eros that he who appears as Antony is no more able to retain this image or appearance of Antony. He had done all this under the fatal spell of Cleopatra who 'packed cards with Caesar'. At this point, Cleopatra's messenger Mardian gives him the false news of Cleopatra's death, at which Antony, full of despair, attempts to kill himself. When he is mortally wounded Diomedes arrives. He is sent by Cleopatra to tell him that she is alive. Diomedes also discloses the fact that Cleopatra is innocent and she has had no previous understanding with Caesar—

> She had a prophesying fear
> Of what hath come to pass; for when she saw—
> Which never shall be found—you did suspect
> She had disposed with Caesar, and that your rage
> Would not be purged, she sent you word, she was dead.
> (4.14.120-24)

Hence, we find that the fatal attraction of Antony and Cleopatra is doomed by human and supernatural elements. Firstly Antony is apparently deceived into believing that Cleopatra has sold him to Caesar which is not true. Secondly he is actually deceived by the false message of Cleopatra's death. It is a Himalayan blunder on the part of Cleopatra, and she has to pay for the error by giving her own life.

Enobarbus is the favourite lieutenant of Antony. He is a straightforward and blunt man who tries to lead Antony in the right direction, for which he is often rebuked and reminded his place. He is not a puritan like Octavius and enjoys merry-making and revelry. He is thoroughly sane and reliable, and also gifted with extraordinary shrewdness and practical intelligence. He is known to call a spade a spade. Appearances fail to deceive him. He can read between the lines and peer into the inner self of a person as once when he corrects Antony's judgment of Cleopatra. Similarly, he understands the extent of Cleopatra's charms, and knows that Antony is sure to return to her, breaking the sacred tie with Octavia—

> **Mec.** - Now Antony must leave her utterly.
> **Eno.** - Never ! He will not.
> Age cannot wither her, nor custom stale
> Her infinite variety. (2.2.237-40)

As he is thoroughly acquainted with Antony's real nature and his fatal attraction to the Egyptian queen, he predicts that his marriage with Octavia will worsen things—

> But you shall find the band that seems to tie their friendship together will be the very strangler of their amity. (2.6.116-17).

His acute observations, his ironic humour, and his loyalty to Antony makes him a distinctive character. After the battle of Actium, when Antony persistently behaves unreasonably he decides to leave him. But the wise and shrewd Enobarbus fails to find any contentment in Caesar's camp and when he is told of Antony's startling generosity in sending his treasures and other gifts he cries in agony—

> I am alone the villain of the earth.
> And feel I am so most. O Antony !
> Thou mine of bounty, how would'st thou have paid
> My better service, when my turpitude
> Thou dost so crown with gold. (4.6.30-34)

Enobarbus is dragged to his death by the load of guilt and remorse. His pathetic end is indeed very moving. On the superficial level he deceives Antony. He appears to be the most intimate and dependable among Antony's followers, yet he deserts him like one deserts a sinking derelict ship especially when he needs him most. On the deeper level one can say—that Enobarbus himself is a victim of appearances. Despite all his shrewdness and common sense, he is devoid of spiritual insight into character. He fails to perceive that man's true character is not restricted to his earthly gains and achievements but lies in his inherent nobility and goodness. He believes Antony to be weak and foolhardy yet he immortalises himself with the genuineness of his passions and his generosity, and Octavius whom he considers invincible is only remembered for his meanness and greed. Loyalty to Antony he has prized and when he is disloyal to Antony, he is disloyal to himself and brings about his ruin.

Ventidius is another one of Antony's commanders. He is successful in his Parthian wars and when Silius advises him to follow the fugitive parthians across Media and Mesopotamia so as to deserve rewards from his great captain Antony, he most tactfully convinces his friend—

> I have done enough. A lower place, note well.
> May make too great an act; for learn this, Silius:
> Better to leave undone than by our deed
> Acquire too high a fame when him we serve's away
> (3.1.12-15)

He is in reality much more intelligent and brave soldier, yet he attributes most humbly his every success to his general. He thinks it wiser to appear submissive and give all the credit of victory to the magic of Antony's name.

Hence, we see that Shakespeare has portrayed quite successfully the vast and colourful panorama of human life, with differing standards of judgment, human natures and moral failures.

6
Julius Caesar

Julius Caesar is one of Shakespeare's Roman tragedies which depicts one of the most catastrophic events in Roman history—the murder of Julius Caesar and its horrible consequences. Both external and internal evidences indicate that the play must have been written about the year 1600. The main source of the play is Sir Thomas North's translation of Plutarch's *The Lives of Noble Grecians and Romans*. Shakespeare has made use of this source closely as far as the general programme is concerned, but has introduced important alternations and modifications in the plot as well as the characters, thus transforming history into effective drama.

On the superficial level it can be said that Brutus is the real hero of the play and the tragedy must have been named after him. But the truth is that in spite of Caesar's death in the Act III, his influence is felt throughout the play. Brutus is successful in destroying only Caesar's body. His spirit comes forward to avenge the murder. It is even more powerful than the living Caesar. Brutus is also mistaken in thinking that he has done an honourable deed in murdering Caesar. In this way he has made his country free from Caesar's tyranny. But he does not know that he has brought upon himself and his country greater evils and disasters than he had sought to avert. There is civil war in Rome and instead of one there are three Caesars—Octavius, Antony and Lepidus. The play depicts the triumph of Caesarism over Republicanism. The Republicans make a wrong choice which causes their destruction and also brings much suffering to the citizens of Rome. The play is about 'jealousy', 'conspiracy', 'murder', 'terrible consequences of the murder', 'civil war' and finally 'the victory of Caesarism'. The play is also about 'ingratitude' and 'treachery'. The tragedy in the play occurs because of misunderstandings, false notions, confused motives, mistaken thoughts and deceptive appearances.

The tragedy *Julius Caesar* depicts the gradual disillusionment and disintegration of an essentially noble man—Brutus. Brutus, as presented in the play, is a philosopher and an idealist, but unpractical having no understanding of human nature and its limitations. In the words of Edward Dowden—"Moral ideas and principles are more to him than concrete realities; he is studious of self-perfection, jealous of the purity of his own character, unwilling that so clear a character should receive even the apparent stain of misconception or misrepresentation. He is, therefore, as such men are, too much given to explanation of his conduct" (Dowden 1970: 283). He is quite out of touch with the realities of life and human nature, yet he has to deal with men in their public and political capacity. As a result, he commits errors after errors, is disillusioned in the end and after undergoing through lots of sufferings dies in the end by his own hands.

In the beginning of the tragedy, Brutus is confronted with the need of making a wrong choice, a choice which appears to be right to him. Both politically and morally, Brutus makes a wrong choice. Brutus commits a mistake in joining the conspiracy. His soliloquy, while he is walking in his garden, reflects that it is not wholly Cassius who persuades him to join the conspiracy, but in reality he himself is persuaded to join hands with the conspirators. Cassius no doubt, represents the facts wrongly and Brutus is easily led by him. A slight provocation by Cassius, by his flattering words, is enough for Brutus to make a wrong decision. His soliloquy depicts his diseased and deceptive thought process. He clearly knows that Caesar has not done anything wrong and harmful for the country in his whole life. He has not been tyrannical till now. To decide to murder a man entirely on the basis of future possibilities is irrational and illogical. His reasoning is inconsistent and illusory—

> That lowliness is young ambition's ladder,
> Whereto the climber-upward turns his face;
> But when he once attains the upmost round,
> He then unto the ladder turns his back,
> Looks in the clouds, scorning the base degrees
> By which he did ascend. So Caesar may.
> Then, lest he may, prevent. And since the quarrel
> Will bear no colour for the thing he is,
> Fashion it thus that what he is, augmented,
> Would run to these and these extremities; (2.1.22-31)

Thus, he commits a murder, a hideous crime, and fancies it a solemn sacrifice done for the country. Brutus does not understand that a dictator like Caesar, who can rule with an iron hand, is the urgent need of the hour in Rome. Brutus' understanding of the nature of the Roman mob turns out to be deceptive. He misreads the people and does not realize that they are hero-worshippers who do not understand republicanism. When happy with Brutus after his excellent speech, the people shout 'Let him be Caesar', thus showing that they do not know the principles of liberty and equality for which Caesar is sacrificed. Brutus' decision to murder Caesar is a political blunder. It is the illusory decision of a theorist, who ought to have remained away from the real world of politics. Big political changes are not possible by a small group. Even if they are brought about, they don't serve any useful purpose. The support of the people is always necessary, which the conspirators lack.

On the grounds of morality also, the decision to murder Caesar is wrong. A murder is always a crime and it is wrong to suppose that anything good can come out of evil. Brutus is faced with a conflict of loyalties—loyalty to his friend and loyalty to his country. Caesar has been to Brutus a good friend and noble benefactor. Caesar has full faith in his honesty and sincerity towards him. When Caesar observes Brutus, the man he trusts a lot, stabbing him along with the other conspirators, he is pained and shocked and falls down with the words—'You, too, Brutus'. Caesar has never expected that Brutus can join those who are opposed to him. Murdering Caesar is surely an act of treachery, betrayal of trust and friendship. Brutus too admits that he loves Caesar, but the reason he assigns to the people for the murder is—

> Not that I lov'd Caesar less, but that I lov'd Rome more.
> Had you rather Caesar were living, and die all slaves, than
> that Caesar were dead, to live all free men? (3.2.22-24)

Antony's testimony to his opponent's patriotism also carries much weight—

> This was the noblest Roman of them all.
> All the conspirators save only he
> Did that they did in envy of great Caesar;
> He only in a general honest thought
> And common good to all, made one of them. (5.5.68-72)

No doubt, Brutus decides to kill Caesar for the good of Rome, but the reality is that he is entirely wrong in his notions of what is good and what is bad for his country. The gradual disillusionment of Brutus is clearly seen. Very soon he realizes that the mob neither considered Caesar a tyrant, nor desired freedom from his rule. Impressed by his speech, the people see a new Caesar in Brutus. Later on when Antony tells them the truth that Caesar was never a tyrant, they support the monarchy and resolve to drive Republicans out of Rome. Thus Brutus' delusion that Caesar has been murdered in National interest is shattered very soon. The glorious image of the democrats is stained by Cassius' acceptance of bribes and earning money through unfair means. Brutus realizes that his fellow conspirators are not the true well-wishers of the nation as he had taken them to be. He is disillusioned to see that they have the same faults in the name of which Caesar was murdered. On the dead body of Cassius he exclaims—

> O Julius Caesar, thou art mighty yet !
> Thy spirit walks abroad and turns our swords
> In our own proper entrails. (5.3.95-97)

Brutus dies disillusioned and disappointed. His last words are—

> Caesar, now be still.
> I kill'd not thee with half so good a will. (5.5.50-51)

He acts with noble intentions but realizes too late that he was wrong. He is doomed mainly because he could not distinguish appearance from reality in almost all the characters around him. He could not see envy, jealousy and malice of the conspirators in doing the evil deed. He misreads his own dear wife Portia and trusts her in telling the secrets of the conspiracy. He could not think of its tragic consequences. He could not correctly understand the deception in Antony's character and rejects the idea of Cassius that Antony should be killed with Caesar—

> And for Mark Antony, think not of him;
> For he can do no more than Caesar's arm
> When Caesar's head is off. (2.1.181-83)

He has a view—

> If he love Caesar, all that he can do
> Is to himself take thought and die for Caesar:
> And that were much he should, for he is given
> To sports, to wildness, and much company. (2.1.186-89)

Brutus could not see his real ability and thus permits him to speak in Caesar's funeral. He has no insight to imagine its terrible consequences because he could neither judge Antony's real worth nor the psychology of the fickle-minded mob. Brutus' disillusionment does not end here. His cherished illusion regarding Cassius' friendship is shattered. His speech about love and friendship with reference to Cassius is—

> When love begins to sicken and decay,
> It useth an enforced ceremony.
> There are no tricks in plain and simple faith,
> But hollow men, like horses hot at hand,
> Make gallant show and promise of their mettle;
> But when they should endure the bloody spur,
> They fall their crests, and like deceitful jades
> Sink in the trial. (4.1.20-27)

Brutus is sad to see that Cassius, who himself is greedy, dishonest and disloyal, blames him of injustice towards him—

> Brutus, this sober form of yours hides wrongs. (4.2.44)

He comes to open rupture with Cassius because he has raised money by questionable means. Cassius tries to hide his faults under the veil of friendship—

> A friendly eye could never see such faults. (4.3.89)

To this Brutus replies—

> A flatterer's would not, though they do appear
> As huge as high Olympus. (4.3.90-91)

Brutus indulges in idealized reflections to support his view that they must move on to Philippi to attack the enemy. In the battle, he gives the word too early, and this is another mistake done by him. Thus he commits mistakes after mistakes and is finally disillusioned in the end. He murders Caesar when he wants to kill his spirit of imperial monarchy, which to his utter frustration, he could not destroy. His wife commits suicide and he is sad to learn that he has sided with people who have envy as their prime motive. Now, he passes sleepless nights. When he is alone in his chamber he is unable to sleep and his inner torments—sorrow, fear and nervousness are externalized by his vision of the ghost of Caesar.

The introduction of ghost in the play is again in accordance with the theme of illusion and reality. Brutus, at first is confused about whether the ghost is real or illusory, whether it is subjective or objective in existence—

> I think it is the weakness of mine eyes
> That shapes this monstrous apparition.
> It comes upon me. Art thou anything?
> Art thou some god, some angel, or some devil,
> That mak'st my blood cold and my hair to stare?
> (4.3.274-78)

But there is no doubt that the ghost of Caesar is unreal and due to the hallucinations of Brutus' agonized soul. In some other plays of Shakespeare, the apparition is real, but in this play, it is a subjective fancy, a product of imagination. He is the only one who sees the ghost. As soon as he recovers his poise, the illusion is broken. The ghost tells him that it is his evil spirit. Brutus now has a sense that all the things he used to consider valuable have in fact wronged him. He has made an unreal division of Caesar the man and Caesar who stands for imperial power. Thus, Caesar's bodiless spirit, which in reality is Brutus' own creation, leads him to his doom. The ghost is the symbol of retribution that overcomes the murderers. It has come to re-establish Caesarism. It's a symbol of justice and punishment. It reveals Brutus' guilty conscience—something which he himself could not acknowledge. Its prophecy depicts the capricious environment of Brutus—the environment which is characterized by treachery, deceit, corruption and betrayal. It's the symbol of Caesar's magnificent presence and Brutus' weakening identity.

Brutus seems to practise the philosophy of stoicism, a philosophy which teaches the principles of being indifferent to pleasure or pain. It's not surprising that he fails so miserably. He actually comes out to be a man of lofty theories, without a true insight into the reality of those theories. The sole purpose of man's life is to seek pleasure and avoid pain. Stoicism preaches exactly the opposite. Brutus could not realize his mistake in following stoicism, which is the reverse of what life ought to be. He is not indifferent to the pain that he ignorantly considers Caesar's power may cause to the Romans. He hates deceptive appearances required by the conspiracy but himself indulges in a more hideous deceit—

> O conspiracy,
> Sham'st thou to show thy dang'rous brow by night,
> When evils are most free? O, then by day
> Where wilt thou find a cavern dark enough
> To mask thy monstrous visage ? Seek none, conspiracy:
> Hide it in smiles and affability ! (2.1.77-82)

He tells his fellow conspirators to maintain a happy countenance so that their intentions are not revealed in their faces—

> Good gentlemen, look fresh and merrily;
> Let not our looks put on our purposes,
> But bear it as our Roman actors do,
> With untir'd spirits and formal constancy. (2.1.224-27)

He stresses on purity and sincerity of motive to do anything, yet he welcomes Ligarius to the conspiracy in spite of knowing that he bears a grudge against Caesar. He has come to know about the dishonesty of Cassius, yet he is ready to take his ill-accumulated wealth to pay his troops. His personal life is attractive. He has a loving wife, faithful friends and loyal servants. All these are the pleasures of life. Even his suicide is an attempt to avoid pain as he understands it. He could not, up to the end of his life realize that he himself wants to reverse his philosophy of stoicism.

Unlike Brutus, Cassius has the ability to take a clear view of facts. He is an opportunity seeking Epicure. While Brutus is honest, simple, straightforward and blunt, Cassius is as cunning as a fox. In contrast to Brutus, he is a shrewd contriver, a practical realist, a crafty politician, and an excellent judge of human character. Cassius starts the conspiracy due to his personal jealousy of Caesar. He himself admits the sharp contrast he feels between his own humble position and the greatness of Julius Caesar—

> And this man
> Is now become a god, and Cassius is
> A wretched creature, and must bend his body
> If Caesar carelessly but nod on him. (1.2.115-18)

However, to get wide support for his evil designs, he poses that he is moved by noble Republican principles. He says that it is good for the people of Rome that he wants Caesar to be dead. He understands that Brutus is honest and honourable, held in high esteem by the Romans. He truly understands Brutus—

> Well, Brutus, than art noble; yet, I see,
> Thy honourable metal may be wrought
> From that it is dispos'd. Therefore 'tis meet
> That noble minds keep ever with their likes;
> For who so firm that cannot be seduc'd ? (1.2.307-11)

Cassius knows that if Brutus takes part in the conspiracy, the deed will look noble and justified. People will justly believe if Brutus tells them that Caesar has been murdered for them and not out of personal reasons. Casca too has a similar view—

> O, he sits high in all the people's hearts;
> And that which would appear offence in us

His countenance, like richest alchemy,
Will change to virtue and to worthiness. (1.3.157-60)

Cassius tries to rouse the feelings of envy and jealousy in Brutus, by flattering him and by using subtle hints—

'Brutus' and 'Caesar'. What should be that 'Caesar'?
Why should that name be sounded more than yours?
(1.2.142-43)

When Cassius feels that it is difficult to rouse jealousy in Brutus, he tries a second way of influencing him by the ideals of liberty and equality. He knows that Brutus can do anything for the public good. Cassius cannot speak out his hatred for Caesar in public, so he lebels Caesar a tyrant. He also appeals to Brutus' pride in his ancestry, and makes him believe that it will be honourable for him to free Rome from the tyranny of Caesar. Cassius has already made the crime appear noble to Brutus. He also forges certain letters as written by the Romans urging Brutus to fight for their cause. Brutus, a simple and credulous man that he is, sees Caesar's passion as a forerunner to slavery and servitude for the Romans. He joins the conspiracy and in this way is misguided by the deceptive motives of Cassius. Cassius faces no difficulty in persuading the other conspirators. He is a cunning and intriguing politician. Antony also could not judge his deceptive appearance—

Fear him not, Caesar, he's not dangerous;
He is a noble Roman, and well given. (1.2.196-97)

It's Caesar who describes him in a proper way—lean, hungry looking, brooding, a prolific reader, a shrewd judge of human nature, and jealous of those who are greater than himself. When he smiles, he simply betrays his frustrated nature. Caesar has the insight to see that such men are very dangerous. Indeed, Caesar's estimate of him comes out to be true. He is the originator and the organizer of the conspiracy, which might have succeeded had he not always yielded to Brutus upon most important questions of policy. While Brutus regards Antony as merely a frivolous young man, given to sports and merrymaking, Cassius has an idea of the real nature of Antony. That is why he suggests that Antony should also be killed along with Caesar—

I think it is not meet
Mark Antony, so well belov'd of Caesar,
Should outlive Caesar. We shall find of him
A shrewd contriver; and, you know his means,
If he improve them, well stretch so far
As to annoy us all; (2.1.155-60)

Cassius does not like that Antony should speak in Caesar's funeral but Brutus does not listen to him. Events prove that he is right in estimating the character and worth of Antony. His views regarding the strategy of war are also right and according to the need of the hour, though Brutus again takes a wrong decision.

Cassius is indeed a remarkable judge of character and situation. He understands things better than others. But the irony is that he himself dies because he misunderstands the situation. Pindarus informs Cassius that Antony has reached his tents to burn them. Cassius asks Titinius to go and see whether the approaching column is friend or enemy. Then he tells Pindarus to stand on the hill nearby to see what happens to Titinius. Pindarus misunderstands the situation and informs him that Titinius appears to have been arrested by the enemy. Cassius thinks that the enemy is advancing towards him and he can be made a prisoner. He asks Pindarus to stab him. Pindarus does as ordered and Cassius is dead. When Titinius comes back with Messala bringing the news of Brutus' victory over Octavius, they come to know that Pindarus had been mistaken. Titinius had actually met friends and not enemies on the way. Messala rightly exclaims—

Mistrust of good success hath done this deed.
O hateful error, melancholy's child,
Why dost thou show to the apt thoughts of men
The things that are not? O error, soon conceiv'd,
Thou nev'r com'st unto a happy birth,
But kill'st the mother that engend'red thee ! (5.3.66-71)

Titinius also laments over Cassius' dead body—

Did I not meet thy friends, and did not they
Put on my brows this wreath of victory,

And bid me give it thee? Didst thou not hear their shouts?
Alas, thou hast misconstru'd everything ! (5.3.81-84)

In this way the deceiver himself is deceived by death.

Apart from Brutus and Cassius the character and speeches of the other conspirators are also important. In Act II, Sc. I, one of the conspirators, Metellus Cimber, on the issue of involving Cicero in the conspiracy, says—

O, let us have him; for his silver hairs
Will purchase us a good opinion,
And buy men's voices to commend our deeds.
It shall be said his judgement rul'd our hands;
Our youths and wildness shall no whit appear,
But all be buried in his gravity. (2.1.144-49)

In the same scene, Cassius expresses his doubt that the prodigies of the wild night and the advice of the soothsayer may prevent Caesar from going to the Capitol. To this, Decius promises to bring Caesar to the Capitol, over swaying any superstitious for bodings Caesar may have. He thinks of a plan—

But when I tell him he hates flatterers,
He says he does, being then most flattered.
Let me work;
For I can give his humour the true bent,
And I will bring him to the Capitol. (2.1.207-11)

After much discussion Caesar decides to stay at home when Calphurnia begs him to do so. When Decius arrives, Caesar tells him that he would not go to the Capitol because Calphurnia has seen in her dream, his statue spurting blood, with many Romans gleefully washing their hands in it. Decius cunningly gives altogether a different interpretation of the dream saying that Calphurnia's dream foretells prosperity and good luck to Caesar. It means that Rome will suck reviving blood, fresh life and vitality from the dictator's deeds. Moreover, the senate has decided to give him the crown, and may change its mind if Caesar does not come. The senators may find it ridiculous to wait till Calphurnia sees a better dream—

Pardon me, Caesar; for my dear dear love
To your proceeding bids me tell you this,
And reason to my love is liable. (2.2.103-05)

Caesar makes up his mind to go to the senate. He asks Trebonius to keep close to him in the senate. To this Trebonius thinks—

...And so near will I be,
That your best friends shall wish I had been further
(2.2.124-25)

When Caesar offers to take, some wine before they leave like friends, Brutus, in an aside, reflects—

That every like is not the same, O Caesar,
The heart of Brutus earns to think upon ! (2.2.128-29)

Thus, all these conspirators show false love and loyalty to Caesar, and in this way prepare a net to trap him.

Antony, when he is first introduced in the play, seems to be a frivolous young man given to games and merry making. He seems to have no care of the state affairs and does not attend to any serious business. Brutus dismisses him as merely a tool of Caesar, insignificant and ineffectual without him. Brutus wrongly estimates him and sees only one aspect of his character. He makes two great mistakes of sparing Antony's life and of allowing him to speak on Caesar's funeral. He errs gravely, and clever Cassius submits to his rash decisions.

Antony is very tactful and as opposed to his outward behaviour, he understands things better and knows how to deal with them. After Caesar's murder Antony sends his servant to the murderers with a tactful message and a request for an interview. He actually wants to set in motion his plan of vengeance for Caesar after he has won over Brutus. His crafty message conveys both his love for Caesar as well as his loyalty to the murderers. He plays on the nobility he knows Brutus possesses and would grant it to him if his petition is adequate. It's not surprising that Brutus is taken in. He promises safety to Antony, even though Cassius voices his misgivings. When Antony arrives, he does not hide his genuine grief at the death of his dear friend Caesar, yet he succeeds in throwing dust in the eyes of the murderers. There is no affectation, no show off in the sentiments that come out of him at Caesar's death. He expresses his love for Caesar even in the presence of his enemies. He praises Caesar and also appreciates the conspirators—

> No place will please me so, no mean of death,
> As here by Caesar, and by you cut off,
> The choice and master spirits of this age. (3.1.162-64)

One moment he shakes hands with the conspirators, the next he turns aside to weep over dead Caesar—

> O, pardon me, thou bleeding piece of earth,
> That I am meek and gentle with these butchers!
> Thou art the ruins of the noblest man
> That ever lived in the tide of times.
> Woe to the hand that shed this costly blood! (3.1.255-59)

Antony very cleverly flatters Brutus to permit him to speak on Caesar's funeral. He appears to be a resourceful opportunist in dealing with the conspirators. Cassius alone understands his true nature but Brutus does not listen to him. Antony truly understands the mob psychology and thus plays upon its emotions. He describes to the mob, Caesar's deep love for them, the brave deeds Caesar has done for the country and reads out Caesar's will. He proceeds very carefully and does not straightforwardly say anything against the conspirators. He presents the truth in a roundabout way—

> Good friends, sweet friends, let me not stir you up
> To such a sudden flood of mutiny.
> They that have done this deed are honourable.
> What private griefs they have, alas, I know not,
> That made them do't; they are wise and honourable,
> And will, not doubt, with reasons answer you.
> I come not, friends, to steal away your hearts;
> I am no orator, as Brutus is;...
> For I have neither wit, nor words, nor worth,
> Action, nor utterance, nor the power of speech.
> To stir men's blood; I only speak right on. (3.2.210-23)

Antony's speech is very touching and emotional. The sentiments that come out of him go straight into the hearts of the people—

For Brutus, as you know, was Caesar's angel.
Judge, O you gods, how dearly Caesar lov'd him!
This was the most unkindest cut of all;
For when the noble Caesar saw him stab,
Ingratitude, more strong than traitors' arms,
Quite vanquished him. (3.2.181-86)

The result is that the mob is incited to revolt. In reality, he proves himself to be a better orator than Brutus. When left alone, he reveals the cunning which underlies the whole performance—

Now let it work. Mischief, thou art afoot,
Take thou what course thou wilt! (3.2.261-62)

Sometimes Antony appears to be immoral, unstable, dishonest, unprincipled and unscrupulous. He appears to be highly ambitious to gain power after Caesar's death. He seems greedy when he alters the will of Caesar and deprives the people of much that he had left for them. His treatment of Lepidus shows his selfishness. He uses him to serve his own purposes and does not want to give him one-third part of the Roman Empire—

And though we lay these honours on this man,
To ease ourselves of divers slanderous loads,
He shall but bear them as the ass bears gold,
To groan and sweat under the business,
Either led or driven as we point the way; (4.1.19-23)

But this is merely a matter of appearance and not the reality. If his methods are unscrupulous, do the men around him are not unscrupulous? He adopts these methods to punish those cruel butchers who have plotted to kill the great leader of Rome. He takes up arms against the conspirators to avenge the death of his friend and a great national leader. He is no less stable, honourable and straightforward than the conspirators. He does not hide his true emotions for Caesar before his enemies. He alters the will of Caesar to raise money for the cause of the battle and not for any personal gain. His decisions in preparing the list of those who are to be killed after Caesar's death show him to be entirely cruel and stone-hearted. But it is an ugly task which is necessary to remove the bad elements from the state. Antony comes in poor light as far as his friendship for Lepidus is concerned. But the reality is that Lepidus is a weak-natured flatterer both in history as well as in the plays *Julius Caesar* and *Antony and Cleopatra*. He is really a subordinate of Octavius and Antony though Shakespeare describes him as one of the triumvirs. Not only Antony but Octavius also uses him as a tool. Antony surely has extremely low opinion about him but he does not make any effort to hide it. Apart from his treatment of Lepidus, Antony is found to be extremely amiable.

The character of Julius Caesar as portrayed by Shakespeare produces the impression that he is a man—cold and calculating, boastful, proud, insulting, arrogant, stubborn and rude. Flavius and Marullus talk about his 'growing feathers'. Cassius complains of his 'becoming a god'. Decius informs us that he is fond of flattery. Casca informs Brutus and Cassius that Caesar has refused to accept the crown offered to him just out of fear of public disapproval. In reality, he wanted to accept it. In this play, we see very little of Caesar's greatness. But one thing is to be remembered that much of the criticism of Caesar comes from the characters that are hostile to him. Cassius is jealous of him and his description of Caesar is veiled in hostility and thus should be rejected. Decius' remark does not truly represent Caesar as it is meant for a special purpose that is to induce Caesar to go to the senate. Moreover, fondness of flattery is a weakness not uncommon in great men, and there is no need to count it heavily against Caesar. In reality, he makes brave attempts not to be tempted by flattery. He is also careful that his weakness does not harm anybody. About Casca's criticism it can be said that Casca is a cynic and it is his habit to find fault with everybody. His character is inconsistent. His only aim is to flatter. He flatters Caesar and is obedient towards him but jeers at him behind his back. He speaks of Caesar with disrespect to Brutus and Cassius and lets Caesar be seen in the light in which the conspirators want him to be seen. He feels that his twisted portrayal of events and characters is enough to convince others and this in fact is true in the case of Brutus and Cassius who want to hear exactly what Casca says. He too, like Cassius, has a discontented rebellious soul, and merely tries to hide it under a facade of good-natured self-control. He is the one who stabs Caesar from behind. He perhaps pretends to be stupid and assumes the garb of blunt honesty to achieve his aim. Cassius truly describes him as—

> So is he now, in execution
> Of any bold or noble enterprise,
> However he puts on this tardy form.
> This rudeness is a sauce to his good wit,
> Which gives men stomach to digest his words
> With better appetite. (1.2.296-301)

On a superficial level, Caesar appears to be extremely superstitious, but he is not so in reality. He believes that Calphurnia will be cured of her barrenness if touched by the runners in the feast of Lupercalia. But this was the accepted belief of all Romans. On other occasions he appears the exact opposite. He dismisses the soothsayer as 'a dreamer' when he warns him to beware of the Ides of March. About his fear of the terrible storm on the morning of his assassination, it can be said that even the bravest man may be frightened by the fury of such a storm and the terrible dreams Calphurnia has seen. But despite Calphurnia's fears and the warnings of the priests, Caesar has the courage to go to the senate to attend the meeting. Thus, we can say that Shakespeare has not deliberately belittled Caesar. For dramatic purposes, Caesar's faults have been emphasized and his virtues have been mentioned only casually. When Caesar boastfully speaks, "Hence! Wilt thou lift up Olympus?" (3.1.73), we feel that the murderers are right in destroying such monstrous pride. But it is only a fleeting feeling. No intelligent person can accept murder as a means to crush pride. Once Caesar is dead, we only hear good about him. Antony presents his true picture before the mob, and very soon the mob realizes that the character of Caesar as represented by the conspirators was fictitious.

Portia's own estimate of some of her qualities turns out to be deceptive. She is very proud of her ancestry and her husband. This feeling of pride lends her a certain self-control, despite her inherent compassion. It is definitely less than what she presumes to have. She thinks of herself as a very strong woman who is much away from the common frailties of women in general. She truly understands the mental disturbance of Brutus after the conspirators' meeting. Brutus tries but could not hide his mental sickness from her. She asserts her right as a wife to know the secrets of her husband. To convince him she says—

> I grant I am a woman; but withal
> A woman that Lord Brutus took to wife.
> I grant I am a woman; but withal
> A woman well reputed, Cato's daughter.
> Think you I am no stronger than my sex,
> Being so father'd and so husbanded?
> Tell me your counsels; I will not disclose 'em:
> (2.1.292-98)

But her self-control and self-discipline does not enable her to bear the terrible strain of knowing the secret of the conspiracy. She is a woman first and then a philosopher. It is not surprising that her self-control slips. Her superficial composure gives way under trying circumstances. On the morning of the carrying out of the conspiracy, when her husband has already gone to the senate, she truly confesses—

> Ay me, how weak a thing
> The heart of woman is ! (2.4.38-39)

No rules of philosophy could keep in bounds her anxiety at the safety of her husband. She is hardly aware what she is saying to Lucius. She has to make great efforts to control her tongue—

> O constancy, be strong upon my side;
> Set a huge mountain 'tween my heart and tongue!
> I have a man's mind, but a woman's might.
> How hard it is for woman to keep counsel ! (2.4.6-9)

Her words reveal the frailty that women have been traditionally associated with. While talking to the soothsayer, she almost gives away her husband's secrets, and then goes indoors to hide her fear and anxiety. Before going inside, she sends a message of her well-being to her husband through Lucius, though she is not well in reality. The manner of her death shows that she could not bear her husband's enterprise any longer.

Suspense and anxiety break her heart and in a fit of madness she commits suicide.

Octavius is the nephew and the adopted son of Julius Caesar. A great reserve of power, courage and determination lies behind the calm and passionless exterior of this beardless schoolboy. Antony calls him 'young Octavius' and crafty Cassius considers him as 'a peevish schoolboy' but in spite of such unflattering epithets and remarks about him, he is a true successor of his uncle Julius Caesar. He is just nineteen years old but assumes a position of power and authority when occasion demands of him. Although less experienced in war as compared to Antony, he assumes leadership and acts as if he were in sole command of war affairs. He is reserved and calm by nature and not a vain babbler. But when he speaks, his every word is decisive. He is an intelligent, cunning and crafty politician who comes at the right moment to reap the fruits of the efforts of others. He is wise enough to think—

> ...for we are at the stake,
> And bay'd about with many enemies;
> And some that smile have in their hearts, I fear,
> Millions of mischiefs. (4.1.48-51)

The speech aptly reflects that appearances are deceptive.

7
Romeo and Juliet

Romeo and Juliet and *Julius Caesar* do not form a group of Shakespeare's plays in the way that the four major tragedies *Hamlet*, *Macbeth*, *Othello* and *King Lear* form. As a group, they stand somewhere between Shakespeare's acknowledged 'great' plays and his lesser works. The early date which is accepted for the composition of this play is 1591. It had been rewritten and revised, and the play, as we know it today, may be dated about 1596. Thus, *Romeo and Juliet*, as it was in its early form, and as it was later recast, should be placed between 1591 and 1596.

The story of *Romeo and Juliet* was found in a Greek medieval romance of the fifth century. Whatever its ultimate origin, it finally became localized in Italy probably in 1303. Though many Italian stories exist, recalling the tragic love of Romeo and Juliet, the names of Romeo and Juliet are not found in the literature of Italy till about 1530, when their sad tale was first told by Luigi da Porto. Da Porto might have heard the story from the Veronese Peregrino, whose story might have its source in the Novello of Masuccio Salernitano. The book was printed in 1476. Various renderings came out of the story after the popularity of Da Porto's novel. One of the well known renderings was Bandello's rendering which was translated into French by Biosteau in his *Histories Tragiques* (1559). The English versions that came out of it were Arthur Brooke's poem *Romeo and Juliet* (1562) and Painter's novel *Romeo and Julietta* (1567). Shakespeare dramatized the material supplied by Brooke and Painter and entirely transformed its spirit.

Romeo and Juliet is a 'tale of love and hate'. The theme is universal as love and hate make the history of the world. The play belongs to the tradition of great love stories like Shakespeare's *Antony and Cleopatra* and *Wuthering Heights* by Emily Bronte. The love theme in the play became so famous that Romeo and Juliet have become a part of folklore. In the beginning of the play, the hero Romeo is in love with the idea of being in love just like Orsino in *Twelfth Night*. His contact with the heroine Juliet sweeps away his false love and replaces it with true sentiments, the sentiments that finally destroy the lovers. Other attitudes to love present in the play are the practical attitude of Capulet, Juliet's father, according to which love is just a business deal, and the attitude of the servants, the Nurse and Mercutio according to which love is purely sexual. Apart from love, the play is also about hatred represented by the rivalry between Capulet and Montague. The death of the two lovers is the price that is paid for the cessation of this feud. The end of the play is tragic because peace is bought at the price of the destruction of innocent lovers. The tragic end of lovers also provides an element of renewal and regeneration which is a special feature of tragedy. Thus 'regeneration' is another theme of the play. *Romeo and Juliet* is no exception in the field of the 'theme of ingratitude'. The central figure of the play is Juliet who shows ingratitude towards her parents who are her well-wishers. In spite of the repeated advice given by her parents, she is reluctant to marry Paris, though at the beginning she gives her consent for this proposal.

Closely connected with the themes of 'love and hatred', 'regeneration and renewal', 'fate and destiny' and 'Ingratitude', is the theme of 'appearance versus reality'. The hero Romeo at first fails to judge the difference between real love and illusory love. He is in love with the idea or illusion of love and not real love. He thinks that his passion, his yearning, his tears for Rosaline depict true love. He is sad to think that in spite of having true feelings of love in his heart, Rosaline is not responding to his love. His friends Benvolio and Mercutio try to make him understand that his passion for Rosaline is hopeless. It's only when Juliet comes to his life that he realizes that his friends were correct. He was simply in love with the idea of love and not real love. After his meeting with Juliet, he is really in love. But unfortunately, the heads of the two houses Capulet and Montague could not understand this true sentiment. The loyalty of Romeo and Juliet to their respective houses would have made them hate each other, but true love in their hearts fuses them together and finally leads them to death. The clash between the two enemies proves fatal for the love and life of Romeo and Juliet. Finally, the life of Verona is purified by love and sacrifice.

The play *Romeo and Juliet* carries us back to a society of Medieval times in Verona, a society which is enslaved by social customs and family feuds, often breaking out into quarrel and fight. Those were the days when love was a passionate thing with the youth, and marriage a heartless business deal with the old. In this play we find a picture of such a society. The Prologue-Chorus tells us about the sad fate of a pair of lovers whose love-story ends in death. Irony lies in the fact that such a tragic play opens as a comedy. Sampson and Gregory are joking and instigating each other to fight with their adversaries. The exchange of vulgar wit between the servants could not hide a certain grim irony which underlines the opening of the play. At this time the two rivals meet. They meet again. The Prince appears in the last scene as in the first. He addresses the Capulets and Montagues, making them understand the scourge that they have brought upon themselves by their mutual hatred including the loss of two of his own Kinsmen.

The element of appearance versus reality can be seen in the character of Romeo, the hero of the play. He is introduced to us as a dreaming lover who is involved in and obsessed by the abstraction about love more than the actual act of love. He is introduced through Benvolio's description of his melancholy and through Montague's sketch of his tears, sighs and his seclusion from the world around him. He is tormented by the cruelty of Rosaline who does not requite his love. She is a matchless beauty to him. He appears to be self-distracted—

> Tut, I have lost myself; I am not here;
> This is not Romeo, he's some other where. (1.1.195-96)

Like Hamlet, who after his father's death, loses interest in the world, Romeo also finds the world and his friends unpleasant. He shuns the company and confines himself in his private chamber and cherishes his fancies about love. In despair he gives himself to abstractions and theorizing—

> Love is a smoke rais'd with the fume of sighs,
> Being purg'd, a fire sparkling in lovers' eyes;
> Being vex'd, a sea nourish'd with loving tears.
> What is it else? (1.1.188-91)

We may think that it is but a fancy, as a young man will be in love when he has no other preoccupation. We do not understand at this moment, whether it is a serious affair at all when Romeo complains that Rosaline is indifferent to him. This time, Romeo is living in a world of illusions, away from the realities of life. He does not himself understand whether he is seriously smitten with love. His discourse with his friend Benvolio puts light on the theme of appearance and reality. When he tells Benvolio that he is sad because he is out of the favour of love, Benvolio replies—

> Alas, that love, so gentle in his view,
> Should be so tyrannous and rough in proof! (1.1.167-68)

He means to say that outwardly love appears to be fair but it is very cruel and harsh in its dealing. It leads a man to a miserable condition. About the love he feels Romeo says—

> Alas that love, whose view is muffled still,
> Should without eyes see pathways to his will !
> ...Yet tell me not, for I have heard it all.
> Here's much to do with hate, but more with love:
> Why then, O brawling love ! O loving hate !
> O anything, of nothing first create !
> O heavy lightness ! serious vanity !
> Misshapen chaos of well-seeming forms !
> Feather of lead, bright smoke, cold fire, sick health !
> Still-waking sleep, that is not what it is !
> This love feel I, that feel no love in this. (1.1.169-80)

Here, we can see an apparent contrast set up between the ready acceptance of the destructive hatred of the two houses by everyone at large and the lovesick Romeo's indifference to its existence. He is away from the harsh realities of life. The artificiality of his feelings is emphasized here. When Benvolio sympathizes with him, he says that Benvolio in an effort to relieve his grief's but aggravates them. The love he shows to him makes his grief worse. Benvolio advises him to forget to think of Rosaline—

> By giving liberty unto thine eyes.
> Examine other beauties. (1.1.224-25)

At first Romeo dismisses the idea by saying that to do so would be to exalt her beauty because no woman in the world can be more beautiful than Rosaline—

> 'Tis the way
> To call hers, exquisite, in question more.
> These happy masks that kiss fair ladies' brows,
> Being black, put us in mind they hide the fair. (1.1.226-29)

Benvolio proclaims that by seeing new beauties at the feast of Capulets, Romeo may forget Rosaline. Romeo agrees to go with him but only to find that Rosaline surpasses all the other beauties of Verona. He has no idea of ever exchanging her for any of the admired beauties of Verona. When he is about to enter the feast, he feels that he is too heavy with illusions of love to dance. But the reality is that Romeo, at the very sight of Juliet in the feast, forgets his old love. He questions himself—

> Did my heart love till now? Forswear it, sight;
> For I ne'er saw true beauty till this night. (1.5.50-51)

Benvolio's desire to cure Romeo of his infatuation by looking at the celebrated beauties of Verona materializes. Romeo's pilgrimage of love begins now. With Rosaline, it was a pilgrimage in theory; with Juliet, it is a venture. The brooding Romeo is dead. His love with Rosaline was a fancy while his love with Juliet is a driving force. A different Romeo appears now, a Romeo who has come out of his seclusion and who climbs the wall of Juliet with no fear of sword. Her kinsmen are no dangers to him. Her eyes are more perilous than the swords of her kinsmen. Before meeting Juliet, Romeo was living out of himself. Now, he is himself in his Juliet. She is his only reality. The rest of the world is to him a passing dream.

Romeo's inner world, after meeting Juliet, is composed and quiet, while Verona is in discord and bloodshed. The outer and the inner worlds are too contradictory to mingle into one. Romeo has a little conflict within himself whereas the conflict between the two families is never ending. At the sight of Romeo in the feast, Juliet's cousin Tybalt rages and fumes but Capulet chides him into peace. Capulet asks him to hide his anger behind a friendly face in order to avoid the bloodshed in his house—

> Therefore be patient, take no note of him;
> It is my will; the which if thou respect,
> Show a fair presence and put off these frowns,
> An ill-beseeming semblance for a feast. (1.5.69-72)

Tybalt leaves the party in anger. His speech here again reflects the theme of appearance and reality—

> Patience perforce with wilful choler meeting
> Makes my flesh tremble in their different greeting.
> I will withdraw; but this intrusion shall,
> Now seeming sweet, convert to bitt'rest gall. (1.5.87-90)

That Romeo's love for Juliet is real can be judged from the fact that after his exchange of love with Juliet in her garden, he runs to Friar Laurence to seek his help. Just before he reaches there, Friar Laurence is indulged in a soliloquy. This soliloquy also has an element of appearance and reality. Talking about the medicinal qualities of herbs and plants Friar says that a thing may appear to be useless and vile but in reality it may be very useful and virtuous—

> For nought so vile that on the earth doth live
> But to the earth some special good doth give;
> Nor aught so good but, strain'd from that fair use,
> Revolts from true birth, stumbling on abuse:
> Virtue itself turns vice, being misapplied,
> And vice sometime's by action dignified.
> Within the infant rind of this weak flower
> Poison hath residence, and medicine power;
> For this, being smelt, with that part cheers each part;
> Being tasted, slays all senses with the heart. (2.2.17-26)

Friar Laurence echoes the words of Benvolio and Mercutio regarding Romeo's hopeless passion for Rosaline. He rebukes him saying that his love for Rosaline was superficial and deceptive. It was a matter of imagination only. His love was rooted in his eyes, not in his heart. He used to weep in vain for her and his tears were false. They had no genuineness in them. Friar is surprised to see that Romeo's passion for Rosaline has shifted over to another lady—

> If e'er thou wast thyself, and these woes thine,
> Thou and these woes were all for Rosaline.
> And art thou chang'd? (2.3.77-79)

Friar gets Romeo and Juliet married on one consideration that the union of the lovers may turn the hatred of the two houses into love and may prove a blessing in the end. Irony lies in the fact that the hostility of the two houses certainly ends but it is along with the end of the lovers themselves.

Romeo means well and does well but fate is against him. His intention to avoid the quarrel between Mercutio and Tybalt involves the death of Mercutio and then of Tybalt. He thinks all for the best but his plans are crossed and he is forced to make a wrong choice. When Romeo hears of the sentence of banishment for him and learns how distracted Juliet is for Tybalt and himself, he draws his sword to kill himself. He loses control over his passions. Friar's speech to calm down his passions is again an example of appearance versus reality—

> Art thou a man? Thy form cries out thou art:
> Thy tears are womanish; thy wild acts denote,
> The unreasonable fury of a beast.
> Unseemly woman in a seeming man !
> And ill-beseeming beast in seeming both !" (3.3.109-13)

Friar says that Romeo appeared to him to be a man of balanced temperament but now his reality is revealed to him. He is bringing shame to his manly figure, his love and his intelligence. His noble figure is melting away like wax. Like an ill-behaving girl he is railing at his good fortune and love.

The contrast between appearance and reality is also found in the character of Juliet. In the beginning of the play she is introduced to us as a submissive and serene girl, under the sway of her parents. She trembles before her mother and fears to face her father. She is ignorant of love and marriage. She can never dream of being in love and oppose her parents in the matters of marriage. Like a docile girl, she hears the proposal of her mother to examine the beauty of Paris. Lady Capulet's speech here again has an element of appearance versus reality. She says that Paris is a precious book of love, but without a binding. He is possessed of beauty external and takes pride to hide beauty internal—

> ...and 'tis much pride
> For fair without the fair within to hide.
> That book in many's eyes doth share the glory,
> That in gold clasps locks in the golden story; (1.3.90-93)

Like an innocent child, Juliet promises to obey her mother in this matter. But after Juliet has her courtship with Romeo, the teenager grows into a ladylove. Love transforms her tenderness into enthusiasm, enthusiasm into passion and passion into heroism. Her passion overrides the bounds of the hostilities of their houses. She shows remarkable strength of character. In order to win Romeo, she can renounce the Capulets. It is a general understanding of mankind that women are of 'weaker vessels'. This understanding has been expressed by Shakespeare at many places. In *Hamlet*, at a place, he says—

> Frailty thy name is woman. (1.2.146)

But Juliet proves this wrong. Though she seems to be quite submissive and docile, yet she has a lot of hidden strength to oppose her parents and to support her lover. She even sacrifices every comfort of life for the sake of her strong desire to get the love of Romeo. Juliet does not believe in affectation or appearances. She is a simple hearted woman who expresses her love to Romeo without any pretension. She fears that by seeing her boldness in declaring her love, Romeo may think her behaviour wanton. But she shall prove truer than those who affect to be coy and distant. On one side, she is very straightforward and open to express her feelings to Romeo. On the other side, she has the capability to hide her true feelings before her parents until it is necessary to tell them. Capulet could never doubt that his daughter can go against him. To Paris, he says—

Sir Paris, I will make a desperate tender
Of my child's love. I think she will be ruled
In all respects by me; (1.4.12-14)

In front of Lady Capulet, Juliet pretends to be weeping over her cousin's death, when in reality, she is lamenting over the banishment of Romeo. Her lamentation over Tybalt's death is an example of appearance versus reality. When Lady Capulet informs her that the villain (Romeo) who killed Tybalt is still alive, she says—

God pardon him ! I do, with all my heart;
And yet no man like he doth grieve my heart. (3.5.82-83)

She shouts that she herself wants to avenge her cousin's death. She can never be at peace until she sees Romeo dead. She feigns all the time to deceive her mother, and seemingly agrees to her mother's plan of poisoning Romeo at Mantua. She says that her heart is so much troubled by her cousin's death that if her mother can get a man to carry a poisoned drug, she herself would mix it to kill Romeo. Her heart is full of hatred for him. But all this is a false show of grief and hatred on her part. She was surely disturbed by Tybalt's death in the beginning but for her, no grief can be more disturbing than the banishment of her lover. Tybalt's death appears to her a trifle when compared to her separation from Romeo. It's only when Capulets inform her about her proposed marriage with Paris that she discloses her true feelings about Romeo. But when she observes that her parents are very much against her wishes to live with Romeo, she again puts on a false appearance. She is deeply hurt to see that even her Nurse sides with her parents. She tries to persuade Juliet to marry Paris since Romeo is banished and can no more come back to her. She begins to justify the point of Capulets by lauding up Paris to the skies. When Juliet sees that there is nobody to stand by her and she is left to her own resources, she decides to seek the help of Friar Laurence. On the face of the Nurse she says that she, having offended her father, is going to Friar Laurence to confess and to be forgiven. As soon as the Nurse turns her back she criticizes her and declares her exact motive in meeting the Friar—

Go, counsellor;
Thou and my bosom henceforth shall be twain.
I'll to the friar to know his remedy:
If all else fail, myself have power to die. (3.4.240-43)

Before Juliet, Paris reaches the Friar's cell to request the Friar to arrange his marriage with Juliet. The Friar who got Juliet and Romeo married in secret, is now in a very complicated situation. What he gets from Paris is that Juliet being too much troubled with grief for her cousin's death, her father wants to hasten her marriage to release her from grief. With great difficulty the Friar hides his inner conflict.

Friar — [Aside] I would I knew not why it should be slow'd. (4.1.16)

In the meantime, Juliet arrives there and meets Paris. She has sense and intelligence enough to put him off by pretending that she has come to confess. When Paris goes away, Juliet describes to the Friar the conflict of her mind. When the Friar finds that she is as desperate as to kill herself, he tells her to go home and pretend that she will marry Paris on Thursday. He gives her a sleeping potion which she is to take on Wednesday night without the knowledge of anybody. By drinking this potion, she will lie in a death like sleep for forty-two hours—stiff and cold. Then she'll be carried to the ancient vault of the family to deposit there as a corpse. When it is time for her to wake up from her pretended death, Romeo, as instructed by the Friar, will come to rescue her. After returning from the Friar's cell, Juliet disguises her feelings with her parents and the Nurse and pretends to accept Paris' suit in the Friar's cell. She begs pardon from her parents and tells them that she has been asked by the Friar to do so. Capulet is very glad to hear that she met Paris at Friar's cell and was nice to him—

Why, I am glad on't; this is well-standup—
This is as't should be. (4.2.28-29)

In his heart of hearts, he thanks Friar Laurence for bringing about such a drastic change in his daughter.

Now, afore God, this reverend holy friar,
All our whole city is much bound to him. (4.2.31-32)

Juliet again tells a lie to the Nurse that she should leave her alone in the night for she has to spend the night in silent prayers. When left alone, she begins to suspect that the sleeping potion given by the Friar might be a poison to get rid of her to keep the Friar free from the stain in her marriage to Romeo. Her mind is full of many other fears and doubts but she dismisses them and drinks the sleeping potion. Next morning everyone finds her dead and gives way to clamorous grief. The Friar calms them down by saying—

> She's not well married that lives married long,
> But she's best married that dies married young. (4.5.79-80)

There is a double meaning in the words of the Friar, which no one perceives. He takes Juliet as one who 'dies married young'. The feigned death of Juliet is an excellent example of appearance versus reality. Irony lies in the fact that while in Verona Juliet is lying dead in her tomb, Romeo is very happy to see a dream that he was dead and Juliet revived him with a kiss—

> If I may trust the flattering truth of sleep,
> My dreams presage some joyful news at hand. (5.1.1-2)

The very next moment, he receives the news of Juliet's death from his servant Balthasar. It's not he but we, the readers know that Juliet can't bring him back to life. But he can surely bring her back to life provided he gets the message from the Friar. Unfortunately this does not happen. Friar John whom Friar Laurence sends with a letter to Romeo, informing him about the feigned death and burial of Juliet, returns without being allowed to proceed to Mantua and deliver the letter to Romeo. Now, Romeo decides to kill and bury himself in the tomb of Juliet along with her. After buying a deadly poison for this purpose, he goes to the Churchyard. He bids his servant Balthasar to leave him alone with his beloved. He tells him a lie that he wants to descend into the vault partly to have a look at Juliet's face and mainly to take from her dead finger a precious ring that he must use for an important mission. But Balthasar, however, keeps in hiding there without the knowledge of Romeo—

Balthasar — [Aside] For all this same, I'll hide me hereabout;
His looks I fear, and his intents I doubt. (5.3.43-44)

In all these situations there is an element of appearance versus reality. The same idea is also reflected when Paris, who has come to the Churchyard to deck the grave of Juliet with flowers, suspects that Romeo might have come here to do some outrage upon the dead bodies. Paris is angry with Romeo because he thinks that Romeo has murdered Juliet's cousin, grief of whom killed the innocent fair creature. He shouts—

Stop thy unhallowed toil, vile Montague.
Can vengeance be pursued further than death? (5.3.54-55)

He could never think for a moment that Juliet's confession and her acceptance of marriage proposal with him was false. He could never think that Juliet is still alive in reality and her death is feigned. He is also ignorant of the fact that Juliet and Romeo are married to each other. He misunderstands Romeo's feelings and his purpose in coming to the grave of Juliet. Thus, failure to distinguish appearance from reality leads him to his doom.

Not only Paris, but Romeo also could not imagine that Juliet's death is feigned and not real. He could never dream that Friar Laurence, who is coming to rescue his beloved, would be just a few steps behind him. This misunderstanding of situation and above all his hostile fate causes his death. He drinks the poison thinking that he is going to meet his beloved in Heaven. He does not know that he is going alone, leaving behind his beloved. When Juliet comes back to her senses, she comes to know the reality through the Friar. She proves her love true by stabbing herself. After the death of Romeo and Juliet, Prince and others throng at the grave of Romeo and Juliet in order to discuss the entire catastrophe. The theme of appearance versus reality can very clearly be visualized in the speech of Friar Laurence. When the Prince says that they should investigate the cause of the mishap, and get hold of the people suspected, the Friar says—

I am the greatest, able to do least,
Yet most suspected, as the time and place
Doth make against me, of this direful murder;

And here I stand, both to impeach and purge
Myself condemned and myself excus'd. (5.3.222-26)

The theme of illusion and reality is also expressed through the character of the Nurse. She is all vulgarity, but she apes the manners of her superiors. She exaggerates all that she copies. She finds nothing sacred in life, no beauty in virtue and no holiness in love. The only thing that is good in her is her sincerity in serving her master and mistress. Juliet thinks her free from all vices and never suspects that beneath her vulgar loquacity she has not a tinge of womanly honour and sensibility. Her love for Juliet, no doubt, is true and she tries to do anything that gives her pleasure. It's only when Juliet seeks her help in her adverse situation, and she advises her to marry Paris that Juliet understands her true nature. She is deeply hurt to find that the Nurse is not what she expected her to be. The same theme is reflected when she plays with Juliet's anxiety to know if Romeo will come to marry her. She puts on a sad appearance on her face. By seeing sad expressions on the face of the Nurse, Juliet's impatience and anxiety know no bounds. She says—

O Lord, why look'st thou sad
Though news be sad, yet tell them merrily;
If good, thou shamest the music of sweet news
By playing it to me with so sour a face. (2.5.21-24)

In another scene, she allows Juliet to think that Romeo is dead, and not Tybalt. The scene in which Juliet is waiting for the Nurse to bring the rope-ladder along with the message of Romeo, conveys a striking contrast and a subtle sense of irony. Juliet observes the Nurse wringing her hands and crying—

Ah, well-a-day ! He's dead, he's dead, he's dead.
We are undone, lady, we are undone. (3.2.37-38)

The Nurse does not tell her at once who is dead. Juliet thinks that it must be Romeo and starts lamenting over her lover's death. When the Nurse clearly tells her that Romeo has killed Tybalt and is banished from Verona, she cries out upon Romeo. Her speech reflects the theme of appearance versus reality. She could not imagine that 'a flowering face' like Romeo's can conceal a 'serpent heart'—

O serpent heart, hid with a flow'ring, face !
Did ever dragon keep so fair a cave?
Beautiful tyrant ! fiend angelical !
Dove-feather'd raven ! wolfish-ravening lamb !
Despised substance of divinest show !
Just opposite to what thou justly seem'st,
A damn'd saint, an honourable villain !
O nature, what hadst thou to do in hell,
When thou didst bower the spirit of a fiend
In mortal paradise of such sweet flesh?
Was ever book containing such vile matter
So fairly bound? O, that deceit should dwell
In such a gorgeous palace ! (3.2.73-85)

To this the Nurse says—

There's no trust,
No faith, no honesty in men; all perjur'd,
All forsworn, all naught, all dissemblers. (3.2.85-87)

The words of the Nurse echo the same theme. She means that no man in the world is faithful and honest. All men appear to be honest and truthful but in reality all are frauds. But when she cries shame on Romeo, Juliet comes back to her senses and strongly opposes her in condemning Romeo. Her cousin might have killed Romeo, and so she forgives him. Juliet feels that her tears are depicting wrong sentiments. She is happy to think that her husband, whom Tybalt might have killed, is alive. Actually, her tears represent the joy and not the sorrow of her heart—

Back, foolish tears, back to your native spring;
Your tributary drops belong to woe,
Which you, mistaking, offer up to joy. (3.2.102-04)

8
Coriolanus

There is no perfect external evidence to decide the date of composition of the play *Coriolanus*. We must depend almost exclusively on 'aesthetic' or internal evidence. By observing the style, meter and diction of the play, we can say that in all probability the play was composed sometime between 1608 and 1610. Shakespeare has borrowed the plot of *Antony and Cleopatra* and *Coriolanus* from a common source that is from North's translation of Plutarch's *Parallel Lives*. Shakespeare closely follows the story of his play as related by Plutarch. Like a dramatist, Plutarch is interested in human psychology exhibited in action. He reveals characters, create lively scenes and writes arresting dialogues. When Shakespeare started dramatising the life of Coriolanus, he found that his work was already done in parts by Plutarch. He had no difficulty in transporting with slight modifications scenes and dialogues from Plutarch into his play.

The present play is a study in 'greatness and nobility', 'patriotism and traitorship', 'pride and egoism', 'class consciousness and casteism'. The hero of the play Coriolanus and his mother Volumnia are endowed with greatness. Coriolanus is a great warrior and a brave soldier and Volumnia is a woman of non-yielding and stubborn will who is not shaken by the greatest adversity and misfortune. In this play Shakespeare draws our attention towards these aspects of their character. While the greatness of Coriolanus lies in his courage and bravery,

Menenius is a character whose greatness lies in his nobility, his love for common people, his lively attitude towards everything, his true friendship for Coriolanus and his ripe wisdom of life. The nobility in the character of Virgilia, the wife of Coriolanus is also highlighted by Shakespeare in this play. A good man is said to be a good man because he has certain virtues. Coriolanus is indeed a good man but he cannot be said to be an embodiment of virtues because he has certain vices also. The greatest vice with him is his pride and it is for the satisfaction of his pride that he can even shun his country. Thus, 'ingratitude' towards one's own country is the greatest drawback that he suffers from. Though pride in personal superiority is the motive force to drive Coriolanus towards heroic deeds on the battlefield it surely is a chief defect of his character. His pride and egoism make him narrow-minded and engendered in him a class-prejudice and hatred for common man. How a great warrior turns out to be a traitor because of his hurt pride is the central underlying idea of this play.

Unlike other tragedies of Shakespeare, the theme of 'appearance and reality' is not easy to find out in this play. Almost all the characters appear to be what they are in reality. The characters do not put on a false appearance to deceive others. After a very careful study of the play, I have discovered some points on the basis of which it can be said that to some extent, the element of appearance versus reality is present in this play also.

So far as the complexity of nature is concerned, Coriolanus cannot be placed side by side with the characters like Hamlet and Cleopatra. He surely possesses varied traits in his character. But these varied traits are not so contradictory as to make him a puzzle like Hamlet and Cleopatra. His appearance is not much different from his reality. His inner self is very much similar to his outer self. Pride is the dominant feature of Coriolanus and this pride makes him both lovable and unlovable. Dowden rightly points out—"A haughty and passionate personal feeling, a superb egoism are with Coriolanus the sources of weakness and of strength" (Dowden 1970: 318).

Coriolanus is a Patrician and is proud of being a member of the aristocratic class. He has pride in his high birth and has a feeling that Patricians as a class are superior in every respect to the Plebeians. Plebeians are born to obey the Patricians and they have no right except the right of obedience. If they revolt against their superiors who are their rulers, they must be ruthlessly suppressed. He hates the Plebeians because they fail to follow that ideal of obedience which he has in his mind. He considers himself as the sole representative of the superior class and wants that the common men should pay him the respect that his class deserves. Closely connected with his class-consciousness is his awareness of personal valour. He firmly believes that he and he alone has the power to defend Rome. Without him Rome is an assemblage of cowards, who cannot stand against their enemies.

Besides being proud, Coriolanus is arrogant, haughty, outspoken, harsh, rude and unpolished. He is unpremeditated in his expression and sharp in his speech. These aspects of the character of Coriolanus are clearly evident to everybody who is in contact with him. But certainly there are some of his features and situations related to him on the basis of which different persons form different opinions about him. Contrasts are surely present in his character, though they are not very prominent and self-revealing. One of the most controversial points about him is related to his patriotism and his sentiments towards his country. In accordance with his habit of boasting off, he, at one or two places in the play, says that he stakes his life in wars just for the sake of his country. His only motive in life is to defend the boundaries and the honour of Rome. He continuously tries to establish this fact in the minds of the natives of Rome. But the reality is that he is wanting in real patriotism. His valour is rooted in his sense of class superiority. He fights not for his country but to uphold his personal dignity and the dignity of his class. Defending country is always a secondary motive for him. The speech of a sensible citizen of Rome is important in this respect—

> I say unto you, what he hath done famously he did it to that end; though soft-conscienced men can be content to say it was for his country, he did it to please his mother, and to be partly proud. (1.1.30-33)

This pride in personal superiority inspires him to do heroic deeds on the battlefield. He renders the highest service to the state till he is kept in high esteem by his fellow Patricians and he is in a position to suppress the voice of the Plebeians against him. But after his exile, the same Coriolanus turns a traitor to his country and leads an army of the Volsces against Rome. The cause of this somersault lies in his hurt pride. Not without a pang does Coriolanus tear himself away from Rome, to whom he has poured his most precious blood. No doubt, he claims the reader's sympathy when he is banished from his country. The feeling is that he has been wrongly treated and punished for more than he deserves. He is certainly a man 'more sinned' against than sinning. But a man who becomes a traitor to his country just because of personal reasons cannot be a true patriot.

Everyone in the play knows that every activity of Coriolanus is governed by pride. But sometimes he pretends to be modest and humble. When Comenius appreciates his bravery and courage, he appears to be very modest—

> Pray now, no more; my mother,
> Who has a charter to extol her blood,
> When she does praise me grieves me. I have done
> As you have done—that's what I can; induced
> As you have been—that's for my country. (1.9.13-17)

He pretends to cross the bounds of modesty when he says—

> You shout me forth. In acclamations hyperbolical;
> As if I loved my little should be dieted
> In praises sauced with lies. (1.9.50-52)

He tries to impress his fellow Patricians by refusing to accept the spoils of Corioli as the price of his valour. But it's surely his pride which makes him do so and not his modesty. He thinks that it is the common soldier, the Plebeians who are greedy of spoils, not he. He ridicules this greed of his soldiers—

> See here these movers that do prize their hours
> At a crack'd drachma ! Cushions, leaden spoons,
> Irons of a doit, doublets that hangmen would
> Bury with those that wore them, these base slaves,
> Ere yet the fight be done, pack up. (1.5.4-8)

How can he, the greatest of the Roman warriors, accept a share in the spoils, which the base soldiers expect? Some critics say that in the end Coriolanus undergoes a remarkable change in his character. He places the interest of people above his own because peace will save the people from misery. When he agrees to establish peace, he has little consideration for himself and he places himself in the power of Aufidius to undo him. To this, it can be said that he offers to make the peace just because his mother wants him to do so. He does this because of family affection and to save his honour and not because he thinks about the welfare of people. He has no love and sympathy for the natives of Rome. But he surely has true love for his family. A contrast between his appearance and reality is seen when at heart he has yielded before Menenius and then before his family members but maintains a stern posture outwardly. We cannot believe that he is above being moved by personal affection or friendship. To Menenius, he says that he cannot be moved by anyone. He does not remember his mother, his wife or his child. This he does just to impress Aufidius and prove his loyalty and faithfulness towards the Volsces. After seeing his mother, wife and son, the conflict of his mind is clearly seen—

> Let it be virtuous to be obstinate.
> What is that curtsy worth? or those doves' eyes,
> Which can make gods forsworn? I melt, and am not
> Of stronger earth than others. (5.3.26-29)

While going through the play, sometimes we feel that we are prejudiced in our opinion about Coriolanus. Coriolanus is not so rude, cold, selfish, mannerless and impolite as people think him to be. He willingly accepts a subordinate command under Cominius. He has filial regards towards Menenius, deep respect towards his mother, pure love for his wife and respect for his wife's friend Valeria. He takes fatherly joy in his son. But Cominius, Menenius, Virgilia, Valeria, Volumnia, his son belong to the privileged class, they are Patricians. Beyond this superior class, his sympathies and imaginations do not reach.

The problem with Coriolanus is that he is sadly wanting intact. He is a soldier, not a statesman. He is a one-sided character who has no gift of self-adaptation. He cannot be other than what he is in his dealings with the people around him. His only sphere is war and he cannot drop in peace-time the austerity and garb of war. He believes in the use of policy and tactfulness in wars—

> Our gates,
> Which yet seem shut, we have but pinn'd with rushes;
> They'll open of themselves. (1.4.17-19)

But he cannot adapt himself to the practical give and take of normal life. This is the main reason behind his strained relations with the Plebeians. By heart, he has great dislike for the common people. But he is not practical enough to put on a fair appearance in front of them. Much against his will, he submits to the established custom of appearing before people in a gown of humility to ask for their votes. But he could not hide his contempt for the people and which the tribunes exploit for their advantage. He mocks at them more than he solicits their votes. Much against his will he pretends to be humble and polite but his hatred for the people is noticed by them—

> I will sir, flatter my sworn brother, the people, to earn a dearer estimation of them: 'tis a condition they account gentle: and since the wisdom of their choice is rather to have my hat than my heart, I will, practise the insinuating nod and be off to them counterfeitly. (2.3.92-98)

When he has to go to the market-place to meet the charges brought against him by the people, it's very difficult for him to be mild. To his mother, he says—

> Why did you wish me milder? Would you have me
> False to my nature? Rather say I play
> The man I am. (3.3.14-16)

He again assumes a polite appearance. But when people call him a traitor, he loses his temper and comes to his true nature. His pride makes him blind to the facts which are as clear as daylight. Underestimating the power of the people, he bluntly says those things which give them an opportunity to banish him from Rome. This absolute nature leads to his death when he boasts of his heroic deeds before the Volsces.

After his banishment, Coriolanus assumes a disguised form so that the natives of Antium could not recognize him. He has a feeling that the city, the widows, the children of Antium owe their misfortune to him. They may revenge upon him by spitting and throwing stones on him. No one recognizes him in his assumed appearance. Aufidius certainly discerns a distinction between his appearance and reality, but even he cannot dream that he may be Coriolanus—

Thou hast a grim appearance, and thy face
Bears a command in't though thy tackle's torn,
Thou show'st a noble vessel. What's thy name? (4.5.60-62)

Unlike Coriolanus, Volumnia is not one-sided. She likes courage and bravery, but she thinks that civic virtues should also be present in a soldier. A man should be able to adapt himself according to circumstances. When she appears in the beginning of the play she appears to be exactly like her son. She is surely the cause of his pride. But as the play proceeds, we feel that she is in many respects different from her son. She advises her son to be guided by policy in his dealings with the Plebeians. She says that she herself has deep hatred for the people, but she can hide her feelings when needed. Coriolanus too should not plainly show the exact nature of his sentiments towards them before he is confirmed in the office of consul. It is binding on him now to speak to the people, not by the prompting of his heart, but in words that merely spring from his tongue—words that are mere utterance, but which his heart disowns. She says that policy and craftiness are necessary in war as well as in peace—

If it be honour in your wars to seem
The same you are not, which for your best ends,
You adopt your policy, how is it less or worse,
That it shall hold companionship in peace
With honour as in war; since that to both
It stands in like request? (3.4.45-50)

Coriolanus is truly her mother's son. His pride, his hatred for the common man, his moving eloquence, his heroic grandeur, his courage and valiantness all he has inherited from his mother. When we observe her in the beginning few scenes of the play, she, like her son, appears to be living in an illusory world of blind power, pride, valour, honour and egoism. She wants her son to be a great soldier and can gladly sacrifice her only child in fighting with his enemies. When she talks of bravery, she appears to be a superwoman. She looks like a woman above all womanly feelings and tenderness. To Virgilia she boldly says—

> ...had I a dozen sons, each in my love alike, and none less dear than thine and my good Marcius, I had rather had eleven die nobly for their country than one voluptuously surfeit out of action. (1.3.22-25)

She feels proud to say that when Marcius was of tender age and soft-bodied and she had no other child than him, considering how honour would adorn him best, sent him to deadly wars which might bring him fame. When we estimate her character in the light of these speeches, it appears that she too, like her son, prefers pride to patriotism. She wants her son to do brave deeds just for fame and honour. Defence of country's honour would be a secondary thing for her. But as the play proceeds we feel that this estimate of her character is not true. She is neither devoid of womanly feelings, nor is she lacking in real patriotism. Her womanly tenderness, her motherly love are clearly seen when Coriolanus is banished from Rome. Now, she is a sorrow-stricken woman. Her son's exile is unbearable for her. She bitterly cries and showers curses on the tribunes and the people of Rome. She takes her son's banishment deeply to her heart.

Unlike her son, Volumnia's patriotism is pure and deep. It's not superficial. Of all the persons in Rome, perhaps, she alone is most sincerely devoted to her country. Her patriotism is revealed when she goes to persuade her son to withdraw his troops from the gates of Rome. She places the interest of her country above every other consideration. It's she who comes forward to defend her country when its fame hangs in the balance. She even kneels down before her son to save her country—

> Down. An end;
> This is the last. So we will home to Rome,
> And die among our neighbours. (5.3.171-73)

Like Volumnia, our estimate of Virgilia on the basis of her first impression turns out to be wrong. She represents a negative process of character-portrayal. She is all that Volumnia is not. She is an embodiment of silent suffering and free from the pride, ambition and egoism of her husband and her mother-in-law. She loves her husband very much. For her, honour and pride are not much significant as compared to the life of her husband. She is more worried about his safety than his honour. When Volumnia says that she would be proud to see her son coming bloodstained from the battlefield after fighting bravely, she cries out—

> His bloody brow ! O Jupiter, no blood ! (1.3.37)

and

> Heavens bless my lord from fell Aufidius ! (1.3.45)

It appears in the beginning that she is a woman who is simply restricted to her family. She has nothing to do with the country she is living in. Patriotism, national honour and country's fame mean nothing for her. But this is not true. She has a strong sense of patriotism because of which she goes with Volumnia to intercede with her husband for the safety of Rome, her country. She is not a timid and cowardly woman. When occasion comes, she can be very bold and outspoken. To her husband, she has the courage to say that if he enters Rome with his army he would have to tread on her womb. She echoes the words of her mother-in-law—

> Ay, and mine,
> That brought you forth this boy to keep your name
> Living to time. (5.3.125-27)

These words are surely an outcome of her love for her country. If she had been a timid and cowardly woman, as she seems in the beginning, she would have sought shelter under her husband to save herself from the fury of war. She would have thought only about the safety of her family. But she, like Volumnia places national interest above personal interest. A proud and egoistic man like Coriolanus highly appreciates the sentiments of Virgilia and Volumnia—

> Ladies, you deserve
> To have a temple built you. All the swords

In Italy, and her confederate arms,
Could not have made this peace. (1.1.207-10)

Menenius Agrippa is a character who is in contrast with Coriolanus. He, unlike Coriolanus, loves the people. He has a tendency to enjoy the pleasures of life without worrying much about anything. With his riper wisdom of life, he knows that extremes are not good for human nature. One should mould oneself according to the need of the hour. He is practical minded and holds the world as the world is. He knows the true nature of the mob and knows how to tackle the furious mob with gentle, persuasive words. When the poor people of Rome come up to revolt against the Patricians because of the scarcity of corn in Rome, he tries to persuade them by relating to them the story of the belly and the other body parts. The story narrated by him depicts the triumph of reality over illusion. In this story, the different parts of the body rebel against the belly with the complaint that she does not toil like them but only stores the food. They have to do all the work. To this the belly replies that the body parts are mistaken in their view about her. In reality, it's she who does the work of storing all the food and supplying it all over the body through veins and arteries. She receives the food which is meant for the use of all the body parts—

Though all at once cannot
See what I do deliver out to each.
Yet I can make my audit up, that all
From me do back receive the flour of all,
And leave me but the bran. (1.1.140-44)

Thus, in reality, each body part receives the best and only dross is left to her. Menenius says that the people of Rome are these body parts and the senators are this kind considerate belly. The senators always do their best for the people. But the mob underestimates them. Whatever benefits they receive, come from these senators. Menenius says that the people are prejudiced in their opinion about the Patricians. They should try to understand them by carefully going into the matters. The people know that Menenius is an honest man and they give him a patient hearing. They are almost half-convinced that their accusation of the Patricians is baseless.

Menenius, the wise old man, understands things better than Coriolanus. He persuades Coriolanus to follow the custom of soliciting the votes of the people in the gown of humility. He truly understands the real nature of both Coriolanus and the people, and tackles them according to their respective moods. On one side, he persuades Coriolanus to behave politely with the mob. On the other hand, he persuades the people to think well about Coriolanus. He tells them that Coriolanus is not bad at heart. He simply lacks the manners of speech. The only fault with him is that he does not hide anything. He is soldier like and unpolished—

> He would not flatter Neptune for his trident,
> Or Jove for's power to thunder. His heart's his mouth;
> What his breast forges, that his tongue must vent;
> (1.1.256-58)

About his own nature he says that he is a friend and not a flatterer of the people. His words and thoughts are same. He is what he appears to be—

> What I think I utter, and spend my malice in my breath.
> (2.1.47)

Tullus Aufidius, the general of the Volsces, is a great soldier like Coriolanus. The proud Coriolanus pays him the highest tribute a soldier can pay to a fellow soldier, when he says—

> I sin in envying his nobility;
> And were I anything but what I am,
> I would wish me only he. (1.1.227-29)

This estimate of Aufidius makes us form very high opinion about him. In the beginning, we think that he is truly a brave man like Coriolanus. But later in the play, we find that his bravery, his courage and valour are superficial only. He is not a real brave man like Coriolanus. Coriolanus may have many defects in his character, but his bravery and courage cannot be put to question. But when Aufidius understands that he cannot defeat Coriolanus in a fair encounter, he decides to employ craft and treachery to achieve his end—

> My valour's poison'd
> With only suffering stain by him; for him

Shall fly out of itself. nor sleep nor sanctuary.
Being naked, sick, nor fane nor Capitol,
The prayers of priests nor times of sacrifice,
Embarquements all of fury, shall lift up
Their rotten privilege and custom 'gainst
My hate to Marcius. Where I find him, were it,
At home, upon my brother's guard, even there,
Against the hospitable canon, would I
Wash my fierce hand in's heart. (1.10.17-27)

Banished from Rome when Coriolanus reaches Aufidius alone and friendless, he welcomes him with open arms. His welcome to his enemy in his trouble rings absolutely sincere. It seems to be the welcome of one great soldier befriending another in adversity. But in reality, this nobility in his nature is corrupted and spoiled by jealousy. Aufidius, who at heart has never reconciled to Marcius, is easily led by the evil designs of his lieutenant. His hidden jealousy again comes up to the surface when he finds that his fame has been eclipsed by his former rival. In Act IV, Sc. V, he speaks words of friendship to Coriolanus in high-flown language—

Thou noble thing, more dances my rapt heart,
Than when I first my wedded mistress saw
Bestride my threshold. (4.5.116-18)

And in the next scene in which he appears (Act IV, Sc. VII), he comes out to be entirely a different man. His jealousy and malice can be rightly seen from his words to his lieutenant—

I understand thee well; and be thou sure,
When he shall come to his account, he knows not
What I can urge against him. (4.7.17-19)

In his heart, Aufidius has decided how to get rid of Coriolanus—

When, Caius, Rome is thine.
Thou art poor'st of all; then shortly art thou mine.
(4.7.56-57)

Aufidius adopts an unsoldierly method to destroy Coriolanus. He makes a secret conspiracy against him. He supports his reason for destroying Coriolanus by saying that he had placed him high and pledged his honour for his sincerity. But Coriolanus, being raised high, has made a lavish use of flattery to secure his position. In doing this, he has even subdued his natural disposition which is always known to be rude, blunt and unbending.

When Coriolanus (Act V, Sc. III) is almost persuaded by his mother to pardon the Roman people, he asks Aufidius if he had been in his place, whether he would have listened to his mother and granted her less than he has granted. To this Aufidius says that he himself is moved by her entreaties and tears. He seems to support Coriolanus. But in front of the lords and the conspirators he says that for a few drops of women's tears which are valued as mere lies, Coriolanus has betrayed the Volscian interests—

> He has betrayed your business and given up,
> For certain drops of salt, your city Rome—
> I say your city—to his wife and mother;
> Breaking his oath and resolution like
> A twist of rotten silk; never admitting
> Counsel CT the war; but at his nurse's tears
> He whined and roar'd away your victory,
> That pages blush'd at him, and men of heart
> Look'd wondering each at others. (5.6.91-99)

Thus, on the grounds of treachery and traitorship, Aufidius and his fellow conspirators kill Coriolanus in the presence of the senators. Coriolanus' fair estimate of him makes us form fair opinion about him. We don't think in the beginning that he can be so cruel towards Coriolanus. His bravery, honesty, patriotism and the love for his country turn out to be false sentiments. They disappear when jealousy, pride, egoism and personal fame come in the way.

The mob of the days of Coriolanus is as fickle, unstable and unreliable as that living in the days of Julius Caesar. It can easily be misled by any powerful demagogue, who can use it as an instrument to serve his personal end. The Tribunes of the people, Sicinus and Brutus are shrewd enough to judge its character correctly and use it to serve their purpose. The interests of the people in the hands of a proud, arrogant and haughty Patrician like Coriolanus can never be safe. Thus, it appears that the Tribunes are justified in asking the people to revoke his election to consulship. But the reality is that they are hostile to Coriolanus long before he asks election on that post. The fame and the popular applause Coriolanus gets because of his bravery, simply fans the fire of their jealousy. They always remain in search of a chance to humiliate and harm him. This chance they get in the election for consulship. They clearly see the opportunity to excite the people against Coriolanus, since it's very difficult for Coriolanus to hide his hatred for the people. The Tribunes clearly notice the hitch of Coriolanus in following the traditional custom of soliciting the votes, which the ignorant people could not judge in the beginning. They poison the mob by misrepresenting the facts—

> Did you perceive,
> He did solicit you in free contempt
> When he did need your loves; and do you think
> That his contempt shall not be bruising to you,
> When he hath power to crush? Why, had your bodies
> No heart among you? Or had you tongues to cry
> Against the rectorship of judgment? (2.3.197-203)

The Tribunes provoke them to refuse to confirm his office of consulship on the point of his pride and old hatred towards the people. They very cunningly mislead the people—

> Lay
> A fault on us, your tribunes; that we labour'd,
> No impediment between, but that you must
> Cast your election on him. (2.3.224-27)

The fickle-minded mob who is wanting in its own judgment, quickly changes its opinion under the influence of the cunning and powerful oratory of the Tribunes. The people create a riot in the city and then laying its blame on Coriolanus, succeed in banishing him from Rome. Sicinus and Brutus are indeed cruel, false, deceitful and treacherous and use patriotism as a means to serve their dirty end.

About their double standards, Menenius says—

> Be that you seem, truly your country's friend,
> And temperately proceed to what you would
> Thus violently redress. (3.1.217-19)

When they have achieved success in expelling Coriolanus from Rome, they themselves discuss their duel policy. Brutus opines—

> Now we have shown our power,
> Let us seem humbler after it is done
> Than when it was a-doing. (4.2.3-5)

The people are thoughtless enough to expel their protector and very soon they have to face the horrible consequence of their folly. They have no clear notion of the danger before them. They do not know whether the danger is real or imaginary. A vague sense of insecurity makes them act in an irrational manner. They betray their want of right judgment in blindly following their leaders. They have no insight to see the malice and jealousy of the Tribunes against the man who is the saviour of Rome in the real sense. They punish their defender, but in punishing him they punish themselves. Dramatic irony lies in the fact that immediately after the popular demagogues congratulate themselves on the peace, order and happiness of the people after the banishment of Coriolanus, comes the news of the Volscian invasion of Rome. The sense of security after Coriolanus' banishment turns out to be illusory. The people could not believe their ears when they hear the news of Volscian army entering Roman territories in the leadership of Coriolanus. They consider it to be a rumour because they can never dream that Coriolanus can be reconciled to Aufidius and attack his own country. It's now that the mob realizes the true worth of Coriolanus. Rome is in peril now and Romans are really repenting for the misdeed they have done out of their failure to judge deceptive appearances.

Thus, after analyzing the characters of this play, we can say that the characters who make a show off of their bravery, courage, patriotism, honesty, sincerity and alike sentiments are in reality insincere, dishonest, cowardly and treacherous. Coriolanus, Aufidius, Sicinus, Brutus and all the citizens of Rome place personal interest above national interest. The characters who remain silent and appear to be lacking in these sentiments truly possess them. Virgilia, Valeria, Volumnia and Menenius all come forward when the fate of their nation is at stake. Their boldness, courage, honesty, patriotism are revealed in the end. Appearances are indeed deceptive.

Like any other Shakespeare's play, Coriolanus can also be analyzed by associating it with theories. The play has been understood by 'Historicist critics' by placing it within the contents of cunning Elizabethan aristocrats like Earl of Essex and Sir Walter Raleigh, constitutional debates about King James, Parliament, Midlands Grain Riots, Politics of London, Ireland plantation and Prince Henry's militant Protestantism. Feminist and psychoanalytic associations pay attention to the body of Coriolanus and his erotically charged relations with his mother Volumnia and Aufidins.

Recent readings of Coriolanus talk about the contradictions inherent in mystifying the royal body and also on the parallels drawn between King James and Coriolanus. The play with its fable of the belly subjects the body politic to scrutiny as a theoretical problem. Corioldanus' obsession with bodies—natural and politic can be placed within the controversy over James' plans to combine England and Scotland into Great Britain. The Union debate moves around the Status of James' body and a number of texts in the first half-decade of his reign focused on this idea. James gave a sigh of relief to the succession anxieties that had troubled England under all Todors (except Henry VIII) as he had two healthy male heirs. His authority strengthened with the spectacle of his body within a fruitful family life. The body politic was used as a tool by the monarch to extract obedience as he referred to himself as the head of the body politic. He made his body the centerpiece of his Union argument by stating that his physical body (body natural) has made possible the Union of England and Scotland. Thus he codified body politic theory in law. The play Corioldanus with its composition in 1607-08, seems to explore the place of King's body in his Union plan and his system of royal patronage by establishing limited parallels between Republican Rome and Jacobean England. It also seems to explore the relationships between the body of the state and the bodies of various characters.

Corioldanus is not only a great tragedy but also a moving meditation on the political temperament. It clearly portrays the dangers for a politician or a leader who fails to understand and establish a relation between the moral need to be true to himself with the practical necessity to be popular. The play is Shakespeare's most political work which has widely been used as a tool for political propaganda. The social context of the play explains why some politicians were interested in the appropriation of the play with the aim of underscoring a particular political agenda at a specific historic time. Shakespeare has demonstrated both sides of the struggle thus proving that his script is adaptable to any political ideology. No wonder that the play is full of betrayals, riddles and contradictions thus establishing a sense of paradox and uncertainty.

9
Timon of Athens

The inimitable Shakespeare is eternally popular as he amuses, instructs and elevates simultaneously. His characters are so varied as Nature itself presenting the dualism and illusion pervading life. *Timon of Athens* has been one of the less popular plays of Shakespeare. Its date of composition too is uncertain. It appears to have been printed in the folio of 1623 where it was called *The Life of Tymon of Athens*. The earliest account of 'Timon' occurs in a digression in Plutarch's *Life of Antony*. There is also an anonymous play entitled *Timon* preserved in manuscript in the Vitoria and Albert Museum.

Timon of Athens is a scrutiny of the disastrous effect of a catastrophe upon an unbalanced mind. It deals with the dramatist's dilemma primarily philosophical as to how to deal with treachery and to receive injuries inflicted on us. One way is that of Timon who turns upon the world with a fruitless and suicidal rage. "The impression which the play leaves is that of Shakespeare's sanity. He could now so fully and fearlessly enter into Timon's mood because he was now past all danger of Timon's malady. He had now learnt to strive with evil and to subdue it; he had now learnt to forgive. And therefore, he could dare to utter that wrath against mankind to which he had assuredly been tempted; but to which he had never wholly yielded" (Dowden 1970: 382).

With this knowledge we proceed to analyse our subject as presented in this play that is 'appearance versus reality' in Shakespearean characters. Timon is thoughtless, prodigal and impulsive. The sudden reversal of fortune in his life is due to his faulty judgment and the flaw in his character. He is slenderly acquainted with his own heart and knows nothing of the hearts and lives of men around him. To him life is a long merry summer. He moves in a dream. He sees in the world around him not reality but his own ideal and an unreal dream based on his false notion that all his friends are as good as himself. He himself is an extremely good-natured man and is ever ready to help his friends and servants. When Ventidius is imprisoned for debt, Timon says—

> Noble Ventidius ! Well
> I am not of that feather to shake off
> My friend when he must need me. (1.1.101-03)

Timon helps him to secure his release from prison. He turns down Ventidius' offer to return the money that had been lent by him—

> I gave it freely ever, and there's none
> Can truly say he gives, if he receives.
> If our betters play at that game, we must not dare
> To imitate them; faults that are rich are fair. (1.2.10-13)

This dialogue shows Timon's thoughtless generosity which leads him to his ruin. He tells Ventidius that the money that he had earlier given for his release from indebtness was freely given. He did not expect any reciprocation of feelings. If those in higher ranks expect a return for their gifts, they have not given in the true sense. We should not try to imitate them because even the faults of the rich persons wear a plausible appearance. They are readily accepted and appreciated by ready flatterers.

Although Timon is acquainted with the common deceitfulness in the world, yet he speaks of it in an unreal and notional manner—

> Nay, my lords, ceremony was but devised at first
> To set a gloss on faint deeds, hollow welcomes,

Recanting goodness, sorry ere 'tis shown;
But where there is true friendship, there needs none
(1.2.15-18)

He feels that ceremony is out of place when there is true friendship. He believes that a friend in need is a friend indeed. He is very complacent and confident of his wealth and considers his friends as an asset. He has no insight to distinguish between a friend and a flatterer. Thus, he is an easy prey to disillusionment and deception in real life. The theme of appearance and reality is the root element of the play. Timon, the leading character in the play, is a victim of deceptive appearances and this deception by his friends remove the scales from his eyes.

Timon who has always found life easy, has given to complacency and excessive confidence. He, in a merry mood, wishes that he was poor if only he could take his friends' help. He believes that he is born to do benefits and what better way there is than to use it for one's friends. There is nothing mean or base about his intentions but his generosity and trust is wasted on undeserving sycophants. The same men who crowded round him desert him when time comes to test their loyalty. He asks his steward, Flavius to have courage and confidence in his friends when the exact situation about his financial condition becomes clear to him—

To think I shall lack friends? Secure thy heart:
If I would broach the vessels of my love,
And try the argument of hearts by borrowing,
Men and men's fortunes could I frankly use
As I can bid thee speak. (2.2.177-81)

He, never in his dream, doubts the sincerity and love of his friends. Flavius knows that his master lives in a dream-world of his own, and is mistaken in regarding the flattering hangers-on as true friends. But he remains quiet. Timon sends his servant, Flaminius to Lucullus, one of the flatterers surrounding Timon, to borrow fifty talents. Lucullus becomes very happy to see Timon's servant for he thinks that he has brought him a present from Timon. But when he learns the real purpose of his visit, he looks grave and serious. He refuses to give the money. He gives

Flaminius three solidaries and asks him to pretend not to have seen him and tell his master that he was not at home.

Another friend of Timon, Lucius expresses shock and amazement when he comes to know through a stranger that Lucullus has refused to lend money to the kindhearted Timon—

> What a strange case was that ! Now, before the gods,
> I am ashamed on't. Denied that honourable man !
> there was very little honour showed in't. For my own
> part, I must needs confess. I have received some
> small kindnesses from him, as money, plate, jewels,
> and such-like trifles, nothing comparing to his;
> yet, had he mistook him and sent to me, I should
> ne'er have denied his occasion so many talents.
> (3.2.16-23)

Yet when the same man is actually approached, he reacts in a manner contrary to his appearance—

> What a wicked beast was I to disfurnish myself
> against such a good time, when I might ha' shown
> myself honourable ! How unluckily it happ'ned that I
> should purchase the day before for a little part,
> and undo a great deal of honour ! Servilius, now
> before the gods, I am not able to do-the more
> beast, I say ! I was sending to use Lord Timon
> myself, these gentlemen can witness; but I would
> not, for the wealth of Athens, I had done't now.
> (3.2.43-51)

Lucius says that he is unable to do what he very much wants to do. He is not in a position to act according to his wish to help Timon. The strangers, who are standing beside him at this moment, truly understand his character. One of them points out—

> Why, this is the world's soul;—and just of the
> same piece
> Is every flatterer's spirit. Who can call him
> His friend That dips in the same dish?
> ....O, see the monstrousness of man
> When he looks out in an ungrateful shape ! (3.2.63-72)

He further generalises—

> but, I perceive,
> Men must learn now with pity to dispense,
> For policy sits above conscience. (3.2.84-86)

Another friend of Timon has a very crafty excuse. When Timon's servant goes to Sempronius's house to borrow money, the latter pretends to be offended and hurt as he has been approached last. He has come to know that Lord Lucius and Lucullus have already denied help to Timon. He says that had he been given the honour of being approached first, he would have readily helped Timon. But under these circumstances he expresses his inability—

> I'd rather than the worth of thrice the sum
> Had sent to me first, but for my mind's sake;
> I'd such a courage to do him good. But now return,
> And with their faint reply this answer join:
> Who bates mine honour shall not know my coin.
> (3.3.22-26)

Timon's servant is astounded at this meanness of a so-called friend who had been nurtured and helped generously by Timon. He points out—

> The devil knew not what he did when he made man politic-he crossed himself by't; and I cannot think but, in the end, the villainies of man will set him clear. How fairly this lord strives to appear foul ! Takes virtuous copies to be wicked; like those that under hot ardent eal would set whole realms on fire.
> Of such a nature is his politic love. (3.3.28-34)

What he means is that man once led by the devil, has surpassed him in treachery and deceit. This man takes a virtuous manner to reach a sinful destination. He appears to be honourable only to fulfill his ulterior motive. He dresses up his sin in holy words. His wickedness is the most crafty and hateful. In the actual world too there in a huge difference between thought, word and deed. The most gruesome acts are performed under honourable pretensions.

Timon is now disillusioned about his friends. The golden dream in which he lived is shattered and his hopes have proved false. "The entire dream structure of his life topples, totters and crashes down. The mirage of universal brotherhood among men vanishes, and he is left in the barren wastes of the world." (Dowden 1970: 387). None of his friends helps him in his need. He curses them for their hypocritical nature—

> Live loathed and long,
> Most similing, smooth, detested parasites,
> Courteous destroyers, affable wolves, meek bears,
> You fools of fortune, trencher friends, time's flies,
> Cap and knee slaves, vapours and minute-jacks !
> (3.6.93-97)

Thus, we can easily steal a glimpse of our theme in the analysis of characters in the play. Timon is a man of strong emotions. He lives in a fool's paradise which ultimately vanishes. If he has little experience of life and human character, he, at least, has nobility of character. He is right in telling his steward—

> No villainous bounty yet hath passed my heart;
> Unwisely, not ignobly, have I given. (2.2.174-75)

He can be accused of providence, not meanness. His goodness and nobility elicits love from his servants. In Act III, Sc. II, even strangers testify to Timon's nobility of nature. But the irony is that such a noble man is a victim of deceptive appearances and due to his sensitive heart he overreacts. He is not a man of action like Alcibiades. His misanthropy is the outcome of his inability to face the hard facts of life. Life turns out to be different from what he had supposed it to be. So he begins to hate mankind. When Alcibiades goes to wage a war against the Athenians, Timon expresses his heartily wish to punish those who have wronged him—

> ...let not thy sword skip one.
> Pity not honoured age for his white beard:
> He is an usurer. Strike me the counterfeit matron:
> It is her habit only that is honest,
> Herself's a bawd. (4.3.110-14)

The play also differentiates between misanthropy assumed by Apemantus and Timon. Apemantus snarls at humanity with his virulent cynicism—

> Immortal gods
> Grant I may never prove so fond
> To trust man on his oath or bond.
> Or a harlot for her weeping,
> Or a dog that seems a-sleeping.
> Or a keeper with my freedom,
> Or my friends, if I should need 'em. (1.2.60-66)

Timon's cynicism has sprung from disillusionment while Apemantus' bitterness is causeless. He is too poor and low born to be deceived by his friends. Hence he puts up the appearance of being a misanthrope living among the rich in Athens, in order to attract attention. In fact he ridicules Timon for his indignant misanthropy—

> Shame not these woods
> By putting on the cunning of a carper.
> Be thou a flatterer now, and seek to thrive
> By that which has undone thee. (4.3.207-10)

Timon hits the nail right on the head when he explains the assumed cynicism of Apemantus. According to him, Apemantus is a slave whom fortune's slender arm never clasped with favour. His pent up frustration and bitterness had made him yearn for the attention and notice of the world. Had he been born among the rich nobility, he too would have been a knave and flatterer. He would also have plunged headlong into loose living and debauchery. Timon is also proud of the fact that he is not like Apemantus. He curses him as the issue of a mangy dog and says that Apemantus ridicules the ways of the world, particularly the ways of the rich, and yet he never misses to attend Timon's parties and banquets. Timon, in his misanthropy, never pretends to be better than others, and never lays claim to any special virtues, while in Apemantus we see that pride and self-complacency with which such cynicism as his is always accompanied.

Alcibiades is the captain of the Athenian army. One of his friends happens to kill an enemy in self-defense. Alcibiades appeals to the senators to pardon his friend considering that the crime was not intentional but accidental. But instead of honouring his pleadings, they banish him from Athens. Alcibiades, therefore, like Timon, has a just grievance against the Athenians. But whereas Timon leaves the city and goes out to live in woods, Alcibiades determines to punish the Athenians for their ingratitude—

> Banishment!
> It comes not ill; I hate to be banished;
> It is a cause worthy my spleen and fury,
> That I may strike at Athens. I'll cheer up
> My discontented troops, and lay for hearts. (3.5.111-15)

Hence Alcibiades stands as a contrast to that of Timon. Like Timon, heatleast, has not been living in a dream. He accepts the pleasures of life and is always ready to endure its pains and misfortunes. He deals with the world as it is. The anger of Timon is barren and it is hushed at last under the sands and the wash of waves. But the active protest to evil by Alcibiades bears fruit. Instead of turning a misanthrope, he strives to set wrong right. He is a man of action. He does not unpack his heart in words and fall a cursing. Not only does he avenge the wrongs, but after his victory he champions Timon's cause and tries to punish those who had betrayed him. Here again our theme of deceptive 'appearances'. When Alcibiades first appears in the play at a party given by Timon, he assures him of his loyalty—

> My heart is ever at your service, my lord (1.2.72)

to which Timon humourously replies—

> You had rather be at a breakfast of enemies than a dinner of friends. (1.2.73)

Apemantus, the cynic, regards him as one of the empty headed sycophants and knaves surrounding Timon—

> Would all those flatterers were thine enemies then, that then thou mighst kill 'em, and bid me to 'em. (1.2.78-79)

But the same Alcibiades who appears to be lacking the nobility of Timon and one of the flatterers surrounding Timon, remains till the end loyal and indebted to Timon. In his conference with the senators of Athens, he makes it clear that he wants to punish not only his own enemies but also the enemies of Timon, and repeats his intention in his acceptance of the terms offered to him by the Senators—

> Then there's my glove;
> Descend and open your uncharged ports
> Those enemies of Timon's and mine own,
> Whom you yourself shall set out for reproof
> Fall, and no more. (5.4.54-58)

Edward Dowden points out—"Although possessed of none of the potential nobleness of Timon, Alcibiades possesses one virtue—that of perceiving such facts as lie within the range of his limited observation. He does not see the whole world, but he sees the positive limited half of it rightly in the main. He is less than Timon, and yet greater; for Timon miserably fails through want of the one gift which Alcibiades possessed" (Dowden 1970: 391).

In a world of selfish, dishonest flatterers Flavius is the only faithful trustworthy man. Flavius looks after his master's property and finances with a rare honesty and efficiency. He dislikes his master's prodigality which would ultimately lead to his ruin, and is always in search of an opportunity to explain his near bankruptcy—

> There's no crossing him in's humour,
> Else I should tell him well, 'i' faith I should.
> When all's spent, he'd be crossed then, an he could.
> 'Tis pity's bounty had not eyes behind.
> That man might ne'er be wretched for his mind.
> (2.1.155-59)

When the actual financial position comes to light and Timon realizes his insolvency, Flavius apologizes for his inability to explain things to him. The tears of Flavius are indicative of his sincere devotion for his master. When Timon's servants leave their master's home, as Timon had already gone to live in the woods outside the city, Flavius gives each servant a small amount of money that he has. Flavius does not desert his master even in adversity. He approaches Timon and offers to serve him still as a servant—

> I beg of you to know me, good my lord,
> 'T accept my grief, and whilst this poor wealth lasts
> To entertain me as your steward still. (4.3.487-89)

In the eyes of the misanthrope Timon, all men are hateful and vicious. He fails to acknowledge the loyalty of Flavius in the beginning. He says that he does not know Flavius. He never had honest man about him. All his servants were knaves because they served meals to villains. He doubts his kindness and honesty—

> But tell me true,
> For I must ever doubt though ne'er so sure,
> Is not thy kindness subtle-covetous. (4.3.506-08)

It is only after the genuine grief and compassion shown by Flavius that he relents and accepts his exceptional honesty in the cruel world. If Timon's friends represent the vicious and mean side of human nature, Flavius is the embodiment of goodness.

The theme of appearance and reality can also be analysed through quotations scattered through the play, beginning with the ironical statement of Timon for painting—

> For since dishonour traffics with man's nature
> He is but outside; these pencill'd figures are
> Even such as they give out. (1.1.161-63)

Timon says that painting greatly resembles man. Since dishonour has degenerated man's nature, he is only his exterior. But there is no deception in these pencilled figures which are the exact semblance of man. Here we find that the words have anomalous ring to them, the augur badly for the future as deception is there in store for Timon. Yet we find that Timon's expression here is not the outcome of his experience of life or thorough knowledge of human nature. He had lived a luxurious, protected and indulgent life. These words are simply uttered as platitudes to show his worldliness and second-hand knowledge of life.

In Act II, a senator summons his servant and commands him to go to Timon and demand the money back which he had lent to him. He has heard of Timon's failing fortunes and the repayment of his loan has become uncertain. He suggests that his servant should assume a very importunate aspect, an appearance of demand—

> Put on a most importunate aspect,
> A visage of demand; for I do fear,
> When every feather sticks in his own wing,
> Lord Timon will be left a naked gull,
> Which flashes now a phoenix. (2.1.28-32)

This quote emphasizes the significance of appearances in the world. Only through appearances one is able to exploit others and convince them. In a world of pretences, genuineness has no value. Although the senator personally respected Timon and was under his obligation yet he asks his servant to demand money in a pretended urgency. Here the position and status of a man has also been proved deceptive as Timon who was shinning like a phoenix would soon be left a naked gull, according to the senator. Hence the social and economic status of a modern man is highly illusive. Indeed the whole life in modern society is conducted through artifice and deception.

In Act III Sc. V, Alcibiades makes futile efforts to persuade the senate to pardon his friend who had killed an enemy in self-defense. The senators had already pronounced death sentence on him and are not prepared to alter it. Their argument is that one who has spilt human blood must die according to the laws of Athens. In vain Alcibiades reminds the senator of the services his friend had rendered to the state. He explains in detail the circumstances in which his friend was compelled to commit the crime in sheer self-defense. To this the senators give the following reply—

> You undergo too strict a paradox,
> Striving to make an ugly deed look fair,
> Your words have look such pains as if they laboured
> To bring manslaughter into form, and set
> Quarrelling upon the head of valour... (3.5.24-28)

The senators accuse Alcibiades of trying to deceive them by convincing them against the ethical code. He is striving hard to present a plausible argument. He has tried to make an ugly deed look fair and honourable. He has taken great pains to present murder as a lawful action, and has given to a quarrel an appearance of chivalry and valour. He cannot succeed in making gross sin look virtue. The senators want to highlight the fact that reasoning, logic and rhetoric can make a bad deed appear good and *vice versa*. Appearances make a lot of difference in a world where what is conveyed and expressed holds a greater significance than the actual truth.

In Act V the Painter and Poet sees Timon in the woods as they have come to know of the gold in Timon's possession. They have always flattered Timon for their own selfish motive—

Poet : Then this breaking of his has been but a try for his friends ?

Painter : ...Therefore 'tis is not amiss we tender our loves to him in this supposed distress of his; it will show honestly in us, and is very likely to load our purposes with what they travail for... (5.1.9-14)

These idle sycophants still plan to double cross Timon, who they believe to be pretending the distress and is actually rich. The cunning parasites approach Timon in order to exploit him with false sympathy and platitudes. They express grief over the fact that he has been deserted by the lords who were frequently benefited by his generosity. They praise his greatness and nobility but it is done only to worm their way into his heart and to get some gold from him. These men are a living examples of the duality. They could go to any lengths to gain material benefit from any man even in a devastated state like Timon's. Even the lords whom Timon asked for help were not ready to believe Timon's actual crisis and took it to be a pretext to test his friends but when they realized its genuineness they backed out. Thus, Timon is hastened to his ruin by these trusted traitors.

The materialist literary criticism developed by Marx says that a particular kind of literature is produced by a particular system of social and economic organization. He interprets and reads many Shakespeare's plays in relation to their societies' different means of material production. His essay on Shakespeare, "The Power of Money in Bourgeois Society" (1944), reads *Timon of*

Athens as less of an age and more of all times. Shakespeare truly portrays the true nature and power of money though this view altogether changes when once wealthy Timon, after losing his fortune, is bound to replace his lavish, luxurious life for solitude and misery in the woods. He exchanges delicious meals for filthy roots and herbs of the forest. His extreme philanthropic disposition gives place to bitter misanthropy. Now, he starts thinking about the wickedness of money and the evils attacked with it. Marx truly terms it as the perversion of the natural order of men and things. Many assumes authority and godly power whereas men occupy backseat.

Bibliography

Alexander, P. (ed). *Complete Works of Shakespeare.* London and Glasgow; Collins, 1951.

Auden, W.H. *Lectures on Shakespeare.* Ed. Arthur Kirsch. Princeton, N.J., Princeton University Press, 2000.

Bailey, John. *Shakespeare and His Plays.* London: Macmillan, 1962.

Barry, Peter. *Beginning Theory: An Introduction to Literary and Cultural Theory.* Manchester University Press, 1995.

Barthes, Roland. *The Pleasure of the Text.* Trans. R. Miller (Hill & Wang), 1975.

Bloom, Harold. *Shakespeare, The Invention of the Human.* New York: Riverhead Books, 1998.

Bradley, A.C. *Shakespearean Tragedy.* London: Macmillan, 1961.

Brown, J.R. *Shakespeare's Plays in Performance.* Penguin Books, Harmondsworth: Penguin Books, 1969.

Burgess, Anthony. *Shakespeare.* Harmondsworth: Penguin Books, 1972.

Cavell, Stanley. *Discovering Knowledge: In Seven Plays of Shakespeare.* Cambridge: Cambridge University Press, 2003.

Charlton, H.B. *Shakespearean Tragedy.* Cambridge: Cambridge University Press, 1948.

Coleridge, S.T. *Notes and Lectures on Shakespeare*. London: Macmillan, 1960.

Dean, F. Leonard. *Shakespeare: Modern Essays in Criticism*. Oxford University Press, 1971.

Dollimore, Jonathan. *Radical Tragedy: Religion, Ideology and Power in the Drama of Shakespeare and His Contemporaries*, 2nd ed. Brighton: Harvester Press, 1984.

Dollimore, Jonathan and Sinfield, Alan (eds). *Political Shakespeare: Essays in Cultural Materialism*. Manchester University Press, 1985.

Dowden, Edward. Shakespeare. *His Mind and Art*. London: Macmillan, 1970.

Edwards, Philip (ed). *Hamlet, Prince of Denmark by William Shakespeare*. Cambridge University Press, 1985.

Granville, Barker Harley. *Prefaces to Shakespeare*. London: Sidgwick and Jacson, 1945.

Haliday, F.E. *Shakespeare and His Critics*. London: Thomes and Hudson, 1947.

Harris, Jonathan, Gil. *Shakespeare and Literary Theory*. Oxford University Press, 2010.

Hazlitt, William. *The Characters of Shakespeare's Plays*. London: Macmillan, 1958.

Hussey, Hourice. *The World of Shakespeare and His Contemporaries*. London: Heinemann, 1971.

Jones, Dr. Earnest. *Oedipus Complex as an Explanation of Hamlet's Mystery*. London: Longman, 1910.

Knight, G. Wilson. *The Wheel of Fire*. London: Methuen, 1960.

Knights, L.C. *Some Shakespearean Themes*. London: Chatto & Windus, 1966.

Lesley, A. and W. Nigel. *Shakespeare in the Changing Curriculum*. London and New York, 1991.

Lerner, Laurence. *Shakespearean Tragedy*. Harmondsworth: Penguin Books, 1963.

Luce, Morton. *Shakespeare*. London: Macmillan, 1930.

Muir, Kenneth. *Fifty Years of Shakespearean Criticism* (1900-1950). London: Macmillan, 1970.

Sanders, Norman (ed). *Othello by William Shakespeare.* Cambridge University Press, 1984.

Shucking, L.L. *The Meaning of Hamlet's Character, Problems in Shakespeare's Plays.* London: Macmillan, 1919.

Sinfield, Alan. *Shakespeare, Authority, Sexuality: Unfinished Business in Cultural Materialism.* London and New York, 2006.

Sodre, I. *Psychoanalysis and Literature.* Paper presented to the British Psychological Society, London, 2000.

Sokol, B.J. *The Undiscovered Country: New Essays on Psychoanalysis and Shakespeare.* London Free Association, 1993.

Spurgeon, Caroline. *Shakespeare's Imagery and What it Tells Us.* London: Cambridge University Press, 1935.

Stephan, Martin and Philip Franks. *Studying Shakespeare.* London: Longman Group Ltd., 1984.

Stoll, E.D. *Art and Artifice in Shakespeare.* London: Macmillan, 1933.

Wells, Stanley. *Shakespeare, The Writer and His Work.* London: Longman, 1978.

Wilson, John Dover. *What Happens in Hamlet*, Cambridge: Cambridge University Press, 1935.

Wise, Inge and Mills, Maggie (eds). *Psychoanalytic Ideas and Shakespeare.* Karnac Books Ltd., 2006.